MW00604868

Your Encore
Retirement Planning Guide:

How To
Balance Time,
Money and Joy

by Glenn E. Frank

Annette,
Have a glorious
next chapter ! !
Glenn

An important note:

"Throughout the book, I mention books, articles, and videos for anyone interested in learning more about the various subjects I discuss. Additionally, I reference resources at my website timemoneyandjoy.com. I don't endorse these works, and I do not intend them to be instructional. You should view and read them with caution and consult experts in the respective fields where you have any questions, or concerns about the content of any article, book or video.

Disclaimers and Warranties:

The author is providing this book and its contents on an "as is" basis and makes no representations or warranties of any kind with respect to this book or its contents. The author disclaims all such representations and warranties, including but not limited to warranties of healthcare for a particular purpose. In addition, the author assumes no responsibility for errors, inaccuracies, omissions, or any other inconsistencies herein. The information provided in this book is for informational purposes only and is not intended to be a source of advice with respect to the material presented. The information and/or documents contained in this book do not constitute legal or financial advice and should never be used without first consulting with a financial professional to determine what may be best for your individual needs.

All rights reserved. With the sole exceptions of users reproducing the "Joy Matrixes" to do personal exercises or by a reviewer who may quote brief passages in a review, no part of this book may be reproduced in any form by an electronic or mechanical means, including information storage and retrieval systems, without permission in writing from the copyright owner Glenn E Frank.

www.timemoneyandjoy.com/

Copyright © 2021 by Glenn E Frank

ISBN: 978-0-578-85814-2

Table of Contents

Preface

Chapter I

Chapter II

Chapter III

Chapter IV

Chapter V

Chapter VI

Appendix:

Dedication

To my wonderful wife, glorious children and everyone else who puts a bounce in their step and a smile on their face every day.

Preface

Setting the Stage: What's Next?

Encore - An additional act given by performers after the planned show has ended – for extended applause!

Curtains up!

Maybe you are reading this as you climb to the summit of your career, perhaps you have already reached that peak. In any case, you are probably beginning to think about the next stage in your life -- retirement. Maybe you plan to indulge in some well-deserved downtime. Or possibly you see a new mountain to conquer. Either way, this next phase in your life presents the opportunity for an exciting new journey.

Let's start our journey together by agreeing to retire the word, "retirement." Why? Think about it. The standard definition for "retire" is 1) Leave one's job and cease to work, typically upon reaching the established age for leaving employment. 2) Withdraw to or from a particular place.

Wow. Talk about negativity. Leave, cease, stop, withdraw. Instead of *stopping* work, I'd argue retirement is about *beginning more meaningful work*. Instead of *withdrawing*, retirement should be about *engaging*. So Instead of using a word that denotes the *end and sleep* to describe the next stage of your life, let's conjure up terms synonymous with fresh starts and/ or new life, words that encapsulate the power to REengage, REcharge,

REjuvenate, REboot, REignite and REjoice. These are words that, rather than suggest a traditional, similar path for all of us, allow each of us the freedom to veer a little bit off-script for our own celebrations. In my book, that word is *"encore."*

The good news is that as you wrestle with defining what encore means for you, you have plenty of company. The number of Americans leaving the 9 to 5 has nearly doubled since the year 2000. Currently, each day approximately 10,000 Americans turn 65, the standard age for retirement. And according to US Census forecasts, that number will reach nearly 12,000 people over the next decade.[1]

With the cast growing every day, "encore" has come to define an exciting post-career stage of life, rife with possibilities. With renewed energy, you may start in one direction and later shift your focus – your encore becomes a journey! And just as vacation travel requires planning to decide how long you will travel, what you can afford, and a destination you will enjoy, the same is true for Your Encore journey. Your future happiness depends on planning now -- considering the tradeoffs you will make between time, money, and joy.

This planning begins at a different point for everyone. Maybe you are a planner extraordinaire. Maybe you bought this book because you have been forced out of your job as a result of the COVID-19 pandemic.

---

1 Kristen Meyers, "Americans Are Retiring at an Increasing Pace," Yahoo Finance, November 21, 2018. https://finance.yahoo.com/news/americans-retiring-increasing-pace-145837368.html

Perhaps our "New Normal" has inspired you to take an unexpected detour on your life roadmap. Or maybe you are simply nearing the end of your career and have more time to reflect.

In all cases, welcome. *I will do my best to guide you in your search. It's going to be easier than you think!*

Before you hire a life coach, attend webinars, or study enlightening books to "find purpose and lead the good life," *it is more important first to study yourself.* Like almost all life decisions, your "encore" happiness will depend on balancing time, money, and joy. *You've been juggling time, money and joy for your entire life.* This balancing act likely underpins every major decision you've ever made. However, as you approach retirement -- your encore -- it's more important than ever to thoughtfully evaluate your choices and make deliberate decisions.

And successfully making any significant change involves first charting your course. So now is the time to think about exactly where all those working hours will go once your current employment ends. There is an exhausting list of possibilities - travel, care for loved ones, charity, church, exercise, part-time work, a new business venture, hobbies, finally learning to play the piano. What combination will make you the happiest? Whatever your interests, the first question you should ask is - Am I going to actively plan my "encore" or just let it happen?

As a professor and financial advisor for over 30 years, I have found that people do not plan their time as precisely as they plan their finances.

This is especially true of those approaching retirement. (Okay, we can't completely banish the word, but we can let "encore" color it.) That is, you may budget $4,650 for yearly travel but fail to consider what you will do day by day once you stop working. *Deliberate "choice management" is critical to your overall well-being when you suddenly have 40+ hours a week to replace.*

At first, all that extra time sounds heavenly. After all, we all have long lists of things we want to do. Who needs structure? Who needs an hour-by-hour schedule anymore? That's often how this next phase begins, chipping away at that long list of to-dos. Then, a few weeks or months in, as the list nears completion or activities become boring, people can become lost. They wonder, *"Why am I getting up today?"* They can only hit so many golf balls, at least straight. Gardening may lose its appeal after a few hours in the sun. Often other people fill their voids for them. "Mary isn't working anymore. Let's ask her to____." And Mary says yes because she hasn't planned her time well enough to say no. *Retirees can drift in a boat without a destination!*

Of course, others kick the retirement can down the road. Despite the financial ability to leave the paid workforce, the emotional capacity to thoughtfully face the next stage in life isn't there. People who cannot leave their jobs may have this innate need to belong somewhere, to matter, and keep working to fulfill those needs. They may rationalize, "I will retire next year... Or I'm earning more money for the kids." If you find yourself in this boat, it's important to *consider whether you are giving up your most vibrant years. Not to decide is a decision!* Continuing to work may be best for you. However, it's important to make that decision consciously and to remember that, if you are married or have a partner, it is crucial to have their support -- you know, *happy spouse happy house.*

Because the opportunity set of activities for that freed up time, your "encore" could be endless, filling in the blanks below can dramatically narrow down the alternatives that would work well in your life. Clarity is key!

- I will fill my available time of _____ hours a week while fulfilling my obligations to others and myself.

- I can do this within my projected budget of $_____ or I need to earn/save an additional $_____.

- I will be excited to wake up every day because_____.

As I see it there are two fact gathering parts to undertake before you start your journey:

Part A - Gain self-awareness.

Part B - Identify and explore your alternatives.

This book is all about Part A – Self Awareness. If you skip Part A, you are effectively taking a trial and error approach. You could easily go the wrong way because you did not know:

- Where your time goes now and where it is likely to go.

- Where your money goes now and where it is likely to go.

- *What truly makes you happy now, and what will likely make you happy in the future?*

In the appendix you will find an extensive list of wonderful organizations designed to help you with Part B - *Identify and explore your alternatives*. The problem is you could spend countless hours in your search and still not be confident you made the right decision. The categories alone can be mind numbing to choose from - Communities to Join, Paid Work, Pro Bono, Volunteer, Entrepreneurship, Social Ventures, Philanthropy. Again. *self-awareness first may be a very effective shortcut!*

In the chapters ahead, you will find:

- Ways to thoughtfully analyze how your schedule fills up and how to "create" more time for what is essential.

- *"Your Post-Career Numbers"* – the cash flow you will need to cover Your Lifestyle Number. If Social Security and pensions will not be enough, what Savings Number is required to fill the void? This momentous dollar total is the point where work becomes "optional!"

- The *"Joy Matrix"* - a straightforward exercise to understand what and who puts a smile on your face -- and then how to make positive changes.

- Exercises to maximize *Happiness Per Hour "HPH" and Happiness Per Dollar "HPD.*
  We all want value for these limited resources!

- Positive Neurochemical Breaks "PNBs" - mood enhancing diversions like the *Smiling Starfish* and uplifting songs.

Navigating future crossroads, which we all know will surface, will be much easier having gone through the Time, Money, and Joy balancing process. That's because your happiness depends on a deeper understanding of what makes you happy. And, significantly, that personal happiness can e enhanced by sharing it with others. The happiest people I know are

ctively engaged with family, friends, neighbors, clients and co-workers.

While some dedicate time to volunteering or give money to formal

harities, others spread joy by small acts of kindness such as holding a

oor open for a stranger or paying for the next customer's coffee in a

drive-through.

So let's raise the curtain on your next act. My wish for your encore?

Thunderous extended applause!

"There is a whole new kind of life ahead, full of experiences just waiting to happen. Some call it "retirement." I call it bliss."

Betty Sullivan

"Street sign: Ho Hum Road & Easy Street In retirement, I look for days off from my days off."

Mason Cooley

Additional Resources:

In addition to this guidebook, on my website timemoneyandjoy.com I share my favorite books, articles, YouTube videos, and Ted Talks on time management, finances, happiness, purpose, changing habits, health. I'm an avid reader and researcher, so the list keeps growing! Fascinating topics include Factfulness, Essentialism, Intuitive Eating, Happy Neurochemicals, *Your Life Purpose in 5 Minutes*, Real Age Calculator, and many more. Warning – these resources can be addictive!

An additional section, *"Guide to Charity and Nonprofit Opportunities,"* offers resources for paid positions, volunteering, and donations.

Many of the links are provided by students, friends, colleagues, and clients. If you have a favorite resource, please share and add to my joy. We are a community! Think of these resources as "travel guides" to help you plan your journey!

Chapter I

Time, Money and Joy: Your Path to Happiness

"The only joy in the world is to begin."
-- Cesare Pavese, Italian poet

have a simple agenda with this book. I want to spread happiness - specially with the "thinking about what follows my career" crowd. And he three-step Time, Money, and Joy process I'll share with you can help ou to do the same.

n a nutshell, the decades I've spent working as a professor and practitioner of financial planning have convinced me that the old cliche hat money doesn't buy happiness is true. Financial independence is just he first step to happiness. However, sometimes we pursue money as if it's he be-all and end-all. That's especially true in my industry.

Looking back on my career, it's not the financial success that has brought happiness to clients and students with whom I've worked. Instead, their joy has resulted from establishing an accord between what they enjoy and value and how they spend their time and money. And, we've found that joy can be turbocharged when it is shared with others.

Before going too much further, I want to distinguish between my use of "joy" and "happiness." I do not use them interchangeably. I'll share a definition of joy I came across in an article, "The Infrastructure of Joy," by Ian Bogost, a contributing editor at *The Atlantic* and the Ivan

Allen College Distinguished Chair in Media Studies Georgia Institute of Technology. Bogost notes that the designer Ingrid Fetell Lee suggests pursuing happiness "from the bottom up, by finding (or creating) moments of joy."

He writes, "Unlike happiness, joy is momentary and small-scale: It comes from intense, momentary feelings of positive emotion. In Lee's view, that makes joy measurable, at least qualitatively. Something that makes you smile or laugh, for example, like watching a dog play or feeling the texture of sand pass through your fingers. Joy is tiny but, over time, these moments lead to happiness."

Lee views joy as "little moments that make us feel alive" that collectively lead to happiness.[2] So, joy is small and often fleeting; happiness, the sum of many joyful moments, is large and, hopefully, long- lasting.

Interestingly, as crucial as joyful moments are to a happy life, synching up how you spend your time and money to achieve joy -- and sharing that joy -- are often missing from the traditional financial planning process. *I've found integrating joy into financial planning requires helping people to make better day-to-day financial decisions and to ensure that they are spending time and money in ways that bring them joy -- and happiness.*

The irony, of course, is that research shows that the pursuit of happiness

2 Ian Bogost, "The Infrastructure of Joy," The *Atlantic*, July 27, 2019. https://www. theatlantic.com/health/archive/2019/06/why-joy-better-happiness/592735/

an be stressful -- and even result in unhappiness.[2] For instance, there's nxiety and plenty of actual work that may not be enjoyable in and of self that goes along with planning an enjoyable birthday party, family acation, or a home renovation. Chasing happiness takes time -- and nat means you have less time to enjoy the present.[4] What's more, our ncreasing use of social media invites us to constantly compare our appiness with that of our neighbors, family, and friends. When we come ıp short, we're unhappy.

've developed a relatively simple and efficient way to pursue happiness hat doesn't require a considerable investment of time or money. And it loesn't devolve into comparing yourself with others. Contrary to the route et out in many self-help books, our quest for happiness will not be a race. t's also likely it won't be a linear journey. Instead, it will be a carefully considered, highly-personalized process that requires you to *sloooow lown* and think about what brings you joy and how you spend your time nd money.

Sing along Go ahead, no one can hear you. (Either link on the next age should work, And if you enjoy this interlude, there will be other opportunities to raise your voice later in the book!)

---

3 Aekyoung Kim and Sam J. Magilo, "Vanishing Time In the Pursuit of Happiness, Psychonomic Bulletin & Review, August 2018.
4 Aekyoung Kim and Sam J. Magilo, "Vanishing Time In the Pursuit of Happiness, Psychonomic Bulletin & Review, August 2018

Simon and Garfunkel's "59th Street Bridge

 www.youtube.com/watch?v=mWBvcJAXwu4

www.youtube.com/watch?v=_QwxTXGSLWQ

♪ ♫ **Slow down, you move too fast...... ♪ ♫**

I hope the lyrics are stuck in your head all day!

his process challenges the financial advice industry's conventional
lanning process. That is, by digging deeper into what brings you joy, we
ake your planning to a higher level -- one that gives you a better chance
f achieving happiness. Given that joy and happiness are often the product
f a tradeoff between time and money, we will focus on crafting an overall
lecision-making framework to guide a more holistic overall plan. The
ime, money and joy juggling act you have performed for prior decisions
vill be thoughtfully addressed for your encore. Some common industry
"Check the Box" questions will not be addressed in this book. These are
questions like how much risk are you comfortable taking in your portfolio
or typical financial questions such as whether you plan to send your
children to private or public colleges.

Instead of making decisions quickly from the gut or following the herd or
financial gurus, the results of a series of simple exercises in this book will
provide you with new insights to help you make decisions that are right
for you. And those decisions will more deeply foster your happiness.

*So often, people dutifully climb each rung of a ladder only to find out that
they placed the ladder on the wrong wall.* Our aim here is to get personal
and be purposeful as we pursue happiness. That could mean moving your
ladder!

Two Kinds of Happiness:

Daily/Fleeting: Things, people, thoughts can generate positive feelings each day.

Deeper/Cumulative: Longer-term, purpose, and accomplishments give life a sense of meaning and create an overall sense of peace and well-being.

Managing the Crossroads

Taking the extra time and care to balance time and money as you pursue happiness is essential when you find yourself at the crossroads between your career and encore. The bottom line is this: As you approach this transition, better aligning your time and resources can make your next stage of life happier.

Almost every decision you make is a tradeoff between money, time, and joy. That holds true no matter the state of your finances or goals. By helping my clients get in tune with themselves, we forge another dimension in planning that creates happiness as they build wealth and transition to their "encores."

Pulling it all together, here's our three-step Time, Money, and Joy planning process:

1. Identify your "Savings Number" where paid work becomes optional. (Your savings number is the sum of a relatively simple equation I'll discuss in the next chapter.)

2. Align your time and money with what you value/love to create joy and happiness.

3. Share your happiness and resources to help others -- and create even greater happiness.

Putting My Process in Context

Before we get started working together, I want to share a little about my unique background as a professor and financial advisor. I'm proud to have played a part in the advancement of the financial planning profession. As the Founding Director of the Masters of Personal Financial Planning program at Bentley University, I designed and taught courses there for more than 20 years.

At the same time, I have also worked for more than three decades as a financial advisor and am proud to have been recognized by *Worth* magazine as one of the country's top wealth advisors every year for a decade from 1998 through 2008. In 2019 I was named *Planner of the Year* by the Massachusetts Financial Planning Association. I am currently the Director of Education at fee-only Lexington Wealth Management in Massachusetts – a partner with Hightower Advisors, a national firm. In recent years I have carved out significant time to conduct Time, Money, and Joy webinar courses for people approaching the end of their traditional working careers-- and for the financial advisors planning with them. And I curate a library of articles and resources at timemoneyandjoy.com that readers of this book often find helpful and interesting. You will also find a list of upcoming webinars at my website.

While my expertise is with money, working with students and clients has required that I learn about time management and psychology. And that has altered how I think about money.

At the most basic level, a financial planner's mandate is "financial optimization." Financial planners work to understand a client's financial goals, factor in all relevant variables, apply technical knowledge and experience and tailor a solution that reflects a client's circumstances.

Yet, while financial optimization is technically financial planning's goal, I've learned over the decades that a client's real goal, and therefore my more specific mandate, is *family happiness optimization*. This involves integrated, objective planning with taxes, college funding, gifting, insurance advice, estate planning and all of the other financial issues facing clients. The big ongoing service is designing and managing a portfolio that grows over a client's working life to reach "the savings number" that will provide a steady cash flow source in retirement. That may sound like a challenge, but getting to the number is the easy part.

Maximizing your happiness from working life throughout your encore takes a bit more work -- and it will be my joy to guide you.

ANOTHER PNB (positive neurochemical break - as promised!)

Yes, I understand you have settled in and are ready to begin our journey but indulge me for two minutes.

I begin every class I teach the same way. I encourage my students to participate in the "Smiling Starfish." In my workshops and classes, we stand up together, strike an open pose with shoulders back, spread our legs a bit, and reach for the stars. And we smile. Looking goofy together breaks the ice and establishes some trust. And from the individual's perspective, striking a version of what social psychologist and author Amy Cuddy refers to as the "power posture" sets you up for success.

So, please get up from the couch or your chair. I'm with you in spirit.

LEGS APART

SHOULDERS BACK

ARMS HIGH

STRETCH

A DEEP BREATH OR 2

AND SMILE

You don't have to keep your arms up for the full time, but you do need to stick with the open stance. And keep smiling. Maybe you can conjure up a happy thought like a child laughing to make smiling easy. If nothing else, think about SpongeBob SquarePants' best friend Patrick --the quintessential smiling starfish. Or that inspiring fearless little girl statue on Wall Street!

As Cuddy's research proves, how we hold our bodies impacts our minds. In other words, by commanding a powerful stance, we feel more powerful. By striking an open pose, we become more willing to try new things. Cuddy says, holding an open stance for two minutes significantly reduces the amount of stress hormones the body produces. Using the open stance to expunge butterflies is an old public speaker's trick. Stretching and deep breathing have obvious physical benefits and smiling releases positive neurochemicals into your bloodstream.

Becoming happier isn't that tough, but it requires a little effort and some new habits. And, from personal experience, I assure you this is a good one. I start every day with the Smiling Starfish. And if I hit a rough patch during the day, I'll repeat it.

So, what if today and tomorrow morning, and every morning after that you resist the urge to grab your cell phone and instead strike up the Smiling Starfish?

Don't fall back on the "I have no time" excuse. I'm talking about two minutes -- such a tiny fraction of your waking hours. If you can keep this routine up for two weeks, there's a good chance it becomes a productive lifelong habit -- at no cost and very little time. Do you see where I am going with this? Keep reading, my friend.

One more time? - ♪ ♫ Slow down, you move too fast...... ♪ ♫

Simon and Garfunkel's 59ᵗʰ Street Bridge song

www.youtube.com/watch?v=mWBvcJAXwu4

www.youtube.com/watch?v=_QwxTXGSLWQ

My husband "The Dedicated Starfish" - Tricia

Chapter II

Big Picture: Thoughts and Trends

"I arise in the morning torn between a desire to improve (save) the world and a desire to enjoy (savor) the world. This makes it hard to plan the day."

— E. B. White

While I work with people of all ages, those actively preparing for retirement are my focus in this book. (Okay. We can't banish the word retirement, lol. But I hope you take my point of planning for more joy with an encore!) Note that middle age provides an advantage if you are settled in terms of career path and family, you can then calculate the "work optional" savings number more realistically.

I also chose this group of 50- and 60-somethings because transition can bring some real unhappiness. At age 50, maybe you have focused your time on work and family and not spent enough time taking care of yourself. Perhaps the kids have graduated from college and are out of the house. Possibly your company downsized, and you are trying to imagine what's next. Perhaps you have suffered the loss of a spouse or are battling an illness. Possibly you've had the good fortune to retire early and have too much time on your hands. In all these cases, you suddenly find yourself on an unclear path to the next phase of your life – Your Encore!

I could argue that the lack of a standard route for what comes next is a positive that gives you the flexibility to choose your path. However, there also can be a lot of anxiety in this transition period -- especially if money is an issue. And your general happiness can take a real hit.

In fact, in *The Happiness Curve: Why Life Gets Better After 50*, Jonathan Rauch, a Brookings Institution scholar, reviewed numerous studies that conclude that most adults' happiness declines through their 30s and 40s and bottoms out in their early 50s -- before increasing again until about age 70.[5] We'll get more into these emerging unchartered waters in future chapters.

So, Are You Happy?

I sense that if you've picked up this book, you are looking to add a little more joy to your life. If that's the case, you are not alone. If at the time you read this, we are still sadly in the "New Abnormal" induced by COVID-19, an increasing number of unhappy people worldwide are searching for happiness as we hopefully move from a "survive" to a "thrive" mindset as vaccines are widely distributed. There has been a recent flurry of discoveries based on synthetic biology, artificial intelligence and energy technologies. The world's technology investment boom may "drive thrive"!

Interestingly, the World Happiness Report from 2019 pinpointed several trends that would thwart happiness during the pandemic: worsening health conditions for many people, declining social trust, and less government

5 Arthur Brooks, "Your Professional Decline Is Coming (Much) Sooner Than You Think, *The Atlantic*, July 2019 .https://www.theatlantic.com/magazine/archive/2019/07/work-peak-professional-decline/590650/

onfidence. Any potential increase in satisfaction resulting from rising

ncomes seems to have been offset by these adverse trends. The 2019

eport added that the US had become a *"mass-addiction society."*[6] That

ncludes everything from substance abuse to social media usage. Before

ou disagree, consider how dependent you are on your cell phone,

specially during quarantine! And then, read on, because there are

trategies for improvement!

Despite the negative trends reported in the *World Happiness Report*,

co-editor John Helliwell offers the positive observation that over seven

years of reporting, there has been a "steady increase in the level and

sophistication of reader interest." He notes that while readers were

previously mainly interested in *how countries ranked* in terms of

happiness, he's noticed an "increasing interest in using the happiness lens

to help understand *what* makes for happier homes, schools, workplaces,

and communities, and to use these findings to help make lives better

everywhere."[7]

That new attention to pursuing and sharing happiness inspires me. I expect

this attitude is particularly strong among people over 50 as they approach

and re-define retirement. I hope this renewed interest in how to find

happiness gives you hope, too -- and motivates you to keep reading.

---

6 World Happiness Report, "Finland Again is the Happiest Country in the World," March 20, 2019

7 World Happiness Report, "Finland Again is the Happiest Country in the World," March 20, 2019 2019.https://worldhappiness.report/news/finland-again-is-the-happiest-country-in-the-world/

And note that while I've tailored the time/money exercises to my over 50 demographic, *the activities and worksheets in the following chapters can also be useful for younger people just starting their careers as well as current retirees.* After all, a little insight into what makes you smile is valuable at any point in your life!

The Bottom Line: In finance and life, your chances of meeting your goals are better if you follow a simple, repeatable process. A quote I like to share with my clients is:

'If you fail to plan, you are planning to fail!'

Benjamin Franklin

TAKE ANOTHER PNB (positive neurochemical break)

I warned you there would be more singing.

Remember the joy you felt as a young driver when your favorite song came on the radio? Or even as an adult! Maybe with your kids in the car? You'd turn it up, roll the window down and cruise along. That's the carefree energy we're after here. *We are all wired for joy*, and the positivity those happy moments create can sustain us through a lot. Even as the pandemic ravaged the globe in 2020, we had constant reminders that seeing the good in others and celebrating small successes amid unfolding tragedy bolstered our resilience to get through the crisis.

Hospital nos across the country often played the Beatles' "Here Comes the Sun" over public address systems during the pandemic. Why not sing along now? Get a little energy to complete the critical exercises in the chapter ahead.

 www.youtube.com/watch?v=xUNqsfFUwhY or

www.youtube.com/watch?v=U_O1QKQCsGs

"Here Comes The Sun"

The Beatles

It is much easier if you Google the lyrics while you sing along.

Chapter III

STEP ONE: Calculate the Savings Number Where Work Becomes Optional

"People say that money is not the key to happiness, but I always figured if you have enough money, you can have a key made."
-- Joan Rivers, American Talk Show Host

It's a cliche that money can't buy happiness, but it's also a proven fact. In 1974, Richard Easterlin, a professor of economics at the University of Pennsylvania and University of Southern California, found that happiness in the US had remained unchanged from 1946 to 1970 despite the significant rise in personal income. This finding that greater affluence didn't translate into greater satisfaction became known as the Easterlin Paradox.

As I tell my clients, although *money can't buy you happiness, it can keep sadness away.* That is, money affords you safe housing, reliable transportation, proper medical care, and healthy food. These things can be the difference between surviving a serious illness - or staying healthy in the first place.

Because the anxiety of an uncertain financial road can be a real drain, let's talk about funding your encore first. Obviously, the amount of money you need to cover all of your essential expenses varies depending on the cost of living where you live and your preferences for these expenditures. Applying what I've learned, advising and coaching so many successful clients can help you identify and achieve your "savings number," or the amount of money you need in your investment portfolio to support your encore. Of course many people are perfectly happy living on less. If a satisfactory lifestyle is covered by Social Security, pensions etc. then you will have no need to save. If part-time work is planned to fill the void you will need to factor in for how many years. For most however some level c savings is a necessity.

The good news is that everybody can get to the savings number by makin; wise decisions along the way. The first step to identifying this target accumulation is to create a budget. Or call it a "spending plan" if you bristle at having your spending "limited" by a budget. The point is that you need to see where you spend your money and identify how much you can direct to your savings target. The feeling of control you get from a budget -- or a spending plan -- can be a powerful financial planning tool.

As always, as you consider your next phase in life, it's important *not to think of a budget as an exercise in frugality but rather as a path to enlightenment and freedom.* While this book is about becoming happier today, some current financial sacrifices *may* be necessary. However, when you make those sacrifices, there is immediate satisfaction -- and even joy - in knowing you are making progress today toward a more secure future tomorrow. That is, reducing unnecessary expenses today may mean you will have greater future control over what to do and when. *Plus, it is entirely possible to actually enhance joy with less spending - see HPD "Happiness per Dollar" exercises in the next chapter.*

et Your Arms Around Cashflow

here are plenty of helpful, budgeting apps. Some have monthly charges. thers are "free" but be prepared for sales pitches. I suggest a simple math st for accuracy: reconcile your budget to your net take-home pay. If you end your net paychecks and do not add to savings or borrow over the urse of the year, then your net pay must equal your living expenses. Of urse that's living paycheck to paycheck. So many people often live this ay when the first step should be to put money aside from each paycheck r their future. There is no better advice to set yourself up for financial curity than to "pay yourself first." Maximize those automatic retirement an contributions at work if you can – at least up to any company match!

ometimes the budgeting exercises illuminate income or spending issues at you need to address. Perhaps you are not making enough to meet our expenses and save. Maybe you are shocked at just how much you re spending on non-necessities. Perhaps there is a big difference between hat you and your partner spend each month. Whether you decide to ddress these issues by boosting your income, seriously cutting your pending, or negotiating with your partner, start with small steps, and ork up to larger leaps. Alternatively, sometimes people are spending ell below their means and are doing without things that would make hem happier. *The point is to know one way or the other how your lifestyle mpacts your future.*

It's been well documented, of course, that money is the number one reaso for divorce. The root of this is that couples' definition of "need" is highly subjective. Over the long term, spending issues become the cause for acrimony and, if not addressed, can lead to alimony!

In contrast, with a collaborative/lighthearted approach where both partner: listen to each other, there can be a happy resolution and an even stronger relationship. I've seen attitudes shift from, "I work hard, and I deserve _____ to *"Gee, now I realize ____wasn't bringing me that much joy and doing ____together is more fun and much less expensive. And that means we will be able to retire comfortably three years earlier."* Honest and regular communication is the key to success. My wonderful wife Kerr and I go on regular "walk and talks" out our back door in a wooded area. It is glorious that we can actually talk without distractions, commune with nature, have a laugh or two, get our hearts pumping, and it's free – perfect HPD!!

Sometimes this work and the ensuing negotiations are difficult and you may feel the need for a professional financial advisor. In the Appendix, I'll offer tips on how you can find some expert trustworthy guidance along this journey. However you travel, it's important to stay positive. Focusing on what's going well in your life and with your finances can reduce current stress and motivate you to plan for the future.

Square one on your journey to greater joy and happiness is calculating your savings number because that number will make it easier for you to make every financial decision.

How to Calculate Your Savings Number:

1. Determine the amount of cash outflow associated with your anticipated lifestyle – housing, food, auto, travel, health care, taxes, gym memberships, etc.

2. List your set inflows from Social Security, pensions, etc. (investment inflows come later).

3. Determine the difference between lifestyle and set inflows. For example, assume you would like to spend $5,000 /month $60,000/ year, and Social Security/pensions will provide $40,000. As a result, you will need to withdraw $20,000 from your investments every year. (this assumes no more paychecks).

4. Assuming a life expectancy of 30 years and using a sustainable 3% annual drawdown, you need a portfolio accumulation of roughly $660,000. (100 divided by 3% = 33 x $20,000 = $660,000). I'll get into the details of this equation in just a bit.

Note that this simple calculation is intended to give you a conceptual sense of "your savings number," not an accurate number. Having a ballpark idea is far better than having no idea at all. I view the number as a starting point on your financial road that makes your journey more certain. All important decisions require adequate analysis. Your savings number is simply a data point.

That said, it's important to realize that many variables can make this guidepost number less accurate. The number of variables in your equation will dictate whether you need to do a more precise calculation on your own or with a financial advisor.

Cheri's favorite HPD (the float not the guy)

Variables that may make this 3% rule of thumb inaccurate

Personal Variables:

- Choppy cash inflow

- Big swings in living expense outflow

- Desire to leave assets for heirs

- Increasing longevity

- Health care or long-term care costs

- Inheritances

- Part-time work in retirement

- Change in payoff date for refinanced mortgage

- Decision to later "spend" the equity in your home

- Taxability on withdrawals for investment and retirement accounts

External Variables:

- Market performance

- Annual inflation

- Income tax changes (federal/state/estate)

Here's a "What's Your Savings Number?" sample table from my financial planning work.

Client:

- A married couple, both aged 66 and retired projected to live until age 95

- No retirement wages, inheritance, pension, etc.

- Living Expenses assume no significant health care costs, including long-term care costs

- No planned gifting to family or charity

Assumptions:

- Annual inflation of 3% for living expenses

- Annual inflation of 2.5% for Social Security benefits

- Income taxes based on Fed 2019 married filing joint rates and 5% state tax

- The Investment portfolio consists of 50% taxable accounts and 50% retirement accounts

- There are no capital gains in the taxable accounts

- An 80% probability that money will not run out

- There is no mortgage on home and home equity is never used for living expenses

Rate of Return represents a compounded annual overall return. As you can tell by this table, the implications of rate of return for "Your Savings Number" can be significant!

Rate of Return	Initial Living Expenses	Initial Social Security Income	Initial "Number"
2%	$60,000	$40,000	$950,000
2%	$120,000	$40,000	$5,200,000
4%	$60,000	$40,000	$750,000
4%	$120,000	$40,000	$3,200,000
6%	$60,000	$40,000	$600,000
6%	$120,000	$40,000	$2,250,000

For illustration, educational purposes only, Please consult your advisor, lawyer, or CPA for details specific to your situation.

Note the repetition of the word "initial" in front of Living Expenses, Social Security income and Number. Obviously, the calculation toward your savings number is an ongoing process. While every number is the result of a unique calculation, there are some generalities that apply:

- The lower the cost for your lifestyle, the smaller your savings number. However, lower expenses and a low number may or may not lead to happiness. You want to spend enough to live well -- or at least well enough and still achieve your dreams. Note, though, that spending patterns developed over decades do not change easily. I can tell a client to spend on a first class vacation because they can well afford it. I chide them with, "You know if you don't fly first-class, your kids will!" However, sometimes that advice goes nowhere because, for example, they have spent all their adult life with the notion that a two-week long vacation is indulgent, let alone flying first class. On the other hand, lifelong overspending may be particularly difficult to change - habits die hard!

- Happiness can require compromise. For example, suppose you are a *minimalist* and your partner is a *maximalist*. You can reconcile in a light-hearted way with humor. If the excessive lifestyle is affordable, try not to let the spending bother you. If it is not affordable, the sooner you both know the implications the better.

- At a certain level of assets/income, the *marginal utility of more is marginal!* Life can certainly get more complicated as your wealth increases. *Plus, you might find that the assets you buy own you!*

Whatever your savings number, when you reach it, work becomes optional. Maybe $1 million is the savings number that gets you a very nice living -- a fine home; a recurring rental in a favorite vacation spot; money to give to family and charity; good medical care; a health club membership, etc. *Maybe a much lower number will work just fine in your life.* Whatever your savings number is, make sure it is large enough that a market drop won't sink you. Tradeoffs are always the key. For example, *if you are able to reduce outflows your savings number is lower which means your encore start date comes sooner!*

How Can You Assess Your Journey's Tradeoffs

Ask yourself:

- What will make me happy?

- How much time can I give it?

- What can I afford?

Ideally, your number is in the sweet spot where you have enough for all you need and want, but not so much that life starts to get too complicated. Push that savings number too high and maybe you begin not to enjoy all that travel and the toys. At some point, planning can get fairly convoluted with family trusts and elaborate estate plans.

Your Withdrawal Rate is Key

Your savings number offers some protection from what is probably your greatest fear -- running out of money and becoming a burden to others. Your withdrawal strategy is the most important variable for a financially successful encore. Withdraw too much early on and you run out of money in your later years. Withdraw too little and you risk not fulfilling your dreams.

So, how much of your retirement portfolio can you safely withdraw every year? The financial advisor William Bengen developed the "4% withdrawal rule" in 1994. Adopted by many advisors, his rule of thumb states you can withdraw 4% of your portfolio in the first year of

...tirement, adjust the amount withdrawn each year for inflation and avoid ...nning out of money over three decades.

...ly general rule of thumb is not to rely on rules of thumb! By definition, ...les of thumb are never meant to apply in all situations. Rather, we ...ould use these standards only as a starting point or guidepost because ...etter decisions result from greater detail, precision and customization.

...significant flaw with the 4% rule of thumb is its annual inflation ...djustment. Outside of healthcare, most retirees won't see their expenses ...ramatically rise. Overall expenses can decline in retirement because ...eople simply have less of a desire to spend as much in their 80s and ...0s.That's why, in all my years as a financial advisor, I've seen very ...ew, if any, clients give themselves a "pay increase" every single year in ...etirement. That said a cost that can rise significantly is health care.

...oing in the opposite direction, another flaw is that Bengen used historical ...narket returns over a 50-year period from 1926 to 1976. Few investors ...xpect returns in the upcoming decades to be as strong. He also used a "set ...t and forget it" approach to asset allocation. That is, he did not adjust the ...nix between stocks and bonds over the years of withdrawals.

...f course, today the traditional 60 stocks/40 bonds portfolio is the ...ubject of great debate. Key questions are: What the overall stock/ bond ...nix should be? How much international versus the US? The good news ...s that inflation is currently low. The bad news is that bond yields and overall expected stock returns are also low. A focus on overall portfolio return and being well-diversified may be critical. "Cautious growth" may be your goal. If you own a home, a fallback position is to somehow tap your equity, buying X number of lifestyle years if the markets are unkind and your portfolio disappears. Furthermore, with hopeful increases in longevity (via finding purpose, meditating, reducing stress, exercising, eating right, socializing...), retirements could last longer. *Bottom line, you want your investment portfolio to last at least as long as you do!*

Therefore, to be safe, I'm more comfortable using a 3% withdrawal rate. And I use that 3% not as a hard and fast rule but as a starting point for discussion and debate. Accordingly, a multiple of 33 times your retirement shortfall (100 divided by 3%) versus 25 times with the 4% rule points to a larger amount to reach "work optional."

Of course, it's essential to be mindful of the need to somewhat adjust your withdrawal amount during a market downturn or a deep recession along the 2008-2009 financial crisis lines. It would be advisable to make a few sacrifices, such as substituting a trip closer to home for a big international vacation. Unless you keep your entire nest egg in cash, you should plan on some loss years because that is the price you must pay for overall long-term higher returns. However, I would not adjust my spending at every market dip or spike up.

Note that per the sample provided, if you keep your portfolio indefinitely in cash-like investments, "your savings number" becomes much larger.

his creates a conundrum that underscores that the price of certainty is very high!

The Three Bears' Rule of Withdrawals

You want to withdraw not too much, not too little, but just the right amount. The goal is to be precise enough in your calculations so you can make reasonable decisions and not have significant surprises.

Your Savings Number is Square One

In summary, your number informs big decisions like: when to retire, whether to work part-time, whether to sell your home, how much to travel, how you choose to help your children financially and/or what you might give to charity. *You should not be making these significant decisions without knowing what your savings number is!*

Of course, there are also decisions you make during the process of calculating your number. Maybe if you continue at your current pace of earning ($80,000 a year), you figure you can retire in five years and maintain your current lifestyle. However, if you are not happy in your job, maybe a far superior plan would be to change careers and make $40,000 a year doing something you love, perhaps working fewer hours, while planning to retire in 10 years. Basically make half as much but work twice as long. And who knows? Maybe your newfound passion continues beyond your new 10 year plan, sort of killing two birds with one stone!

Whatever your path, your number can curtail your stress. I've had clients complain that their recently-retired-with-way-too-much-time-on-their-hands spouse runs around turning off lights to cut the electric bill. A phone message like this is not unusual: *"Glenn, can you call John and tell him he needs to go back to work. He is driving me crazy with his constant worry - turning off lights, checking our investments every hour. He has way too much time on his hands and was happier working"*. Other clients although they have more than enough money to support themselves, relate to driving down the road and seeing themselves in a ditch, penniless. Those fears are powerful, so having the math on your side to support your future decisions is a real stress reducer, a crucial first step to a happy retirement.

Are you having difficulty with these calculations?

Consider a free registration at lifeplanningforyou.com "Retirement Calculator". BERT - Back of the Envelope Retirement Tool solves for how much you can spend based on what you have saved. This chapter is the opposite "how much you need to save to spend a given amount". Not to worry - you can easily play with BERT to get to your savings number. BERT factors in part-time pay, equity in your home and inheritance. Again, do not assume any real accuracy with any calculator and seek professional guidance when needed. Ballparks are very helpful however!

As an aside I heartily endorse George Kinder, his institute, his army of RLPs - Registered Life Planners and his books including "Life Planning for You". I speak from personal experience as I have my own very talented Kinder trained RLP. The only thing more enjoyable than talking about yourself is having someone else talk about you who really cares!

The Bottom Line: There are many variables outside of your control but an estimate of your savings number is far better than a guess -- and much better than nothing at all.

Homework: Financial Enlightenment

- Calculate your current "Work Optional" Savings Number (roughly at least).

- Review your cash inflows thinking about the impact on your happiness.

- Review your cash outflows thinking about the impact on your happiness.

If these cash flow reviews trigger changes, recalculate your Savings Number.

Note that there is "Choice Management" homework at the end of the next chapter. Conclusions you reach in doing this homework may have financial implications – you may need to come back and update your Savings Number. My overall process can be iterative as the steps are interdependent. You will find however, that the clarity provided is worth the effort!

AFTER THE MONEY CHAPTER TIME FOR 3 PNB's!

SMILING STARFISH

LEGS APART

SHOULDERS BACK

ARMS OPEN

STRETCH

DEEP BREATHS

AND SMILE

And if you feel like singing.

 www.youtube.com/watch?v=CWzrABouyeE or

www.youtube.com/watch?v=A3yCcXgbKrE

♪ ♫ What a Wonderful World ♪ ♫

by Louis Armstrong

A laugh or 2...

Accident insurance claim forms ask for a brief statement about how the accident happened. The combination of the finger pointing instinct and the small spaces provided on the forms can lead to some curiously phrased explanations.

"A pedestrian hit me and went under my car."

"Coming home, I drove into the wrong house and collided with a tree don't have."

"I saw the slow-moving, sad-faced old gentleman as he bounced off the hood of my car."

"The indirect cause of this accident was a little guy in a small car with a big mouth."

"I was thrown from my car as it left the road. I was later found in a ditch by some stray cows."

www.rinkworks.com/said/insurance.shtml **for more.**

Chapter IV

STEP TWO: Align How You Spend TIME and MONEY to Find JOY

This is the "carefully juggle so no balls are dropped" chapter. I strongly suggest you read this chapter slowly and thoughtfully. Take plenty of time to do the exercises and homework. Chapter IV could be transformational - it is up to you!

"Happiness depends on ourselves."
-- Aristotle,
Greek philosopher and "Father of Western Philosophy."

Evaluate Your Activities

Now that you know your withdrawal and savings numbers, let's turn to some decision-making exercises. These will help to uncover what brings you joy and whether you are spending your time and money in a purposeful way, one that brings you happiness. It is important as you embark on your "Encore" journey to understand what brings you happiness now and why. What is it about a particular activity that ultimately puts a bounce in your step? *With this knowledge, you can more wisely choose the initial path that is best for you, rather than trial and ERROR. You would hate to make a mistake that took you years to realize!*

For example, the major decision to leave your job to launch the business you always dreamed about calls for some serious introspection. The "why" is critical! Perhaps after being an employee for all of those years, your

"Why", your motivator, might relate to building something that you can control or, something where the profits are yours or, greater opportunities for your talents to shine. There may be other joyous things in your life however, that could be sacrificed. You might find that the new business comes with unexpected stress, work friends have now been replaced by employees and customers for whom you are now "responsible for". You become an administrator, not doing the enjoyable essence of the business. In starting a new venture, the time has vanished for planned exercise, hobbies, volunteering, family and all of those walks on the beach you wer planning. Plus, you are now in too deep financially to change course and worse yet, there is now a serious strain on your marriage. Then again, the new "adventure" could be the best decision you ever made. *The point is don't be surprised. Be proactive and plan!*

Traditional financial planning work often starts with the simple question, "What are my financial goals?" and involves plenty of detail and follow-up. Yet, throughout the planning process, there is not enough effort to discover if clients are actually spending time and money working toward their true, overall maximize family happiness goals. Therefore, by the time retirement arrives, it's no surprise that the industry has turned out golfers who don't golf, world travelers who fail to go on vacation, etc.

Discussing goals should be subsequent to exploring what brings you joy and how you can cultivate happiness. Reading Dan Buettner's *The Blue Zones of Happiness* inspired me to ask myself some important questions at I'm betting many of you have not taken the time to ask:

- What makes me happy? Why?
- What activities absorb me? *("Flow" or "In the Zone")*
- What brings me meaning?
- How do I spend my time?
- Can I reconcile any differences?

What does my happiness cost, in terms of time and money?

I've since shared these questions with financial planning clients to encourage some alternative thinking. In a world driven by consumerism, we suffer from an insatiable "more is better" philosophy. But, rather than work for more, how much do we really need? Does the pursuit of more money take time away from activities that make us happy? Does gratification come from the pursuit of money or the actual money?

As you can guess from this book's subtitle, I believe time, money and joy are almost always intertwined, invariably in tension with each other and need to be "juggled"! The high-paying job as a corporate attorney may not be fulfilling and it pulls you away from your passion for spending time at the ocean, but you have bills to pay, children to educate and you don't want to work forever. On the other end of the spectrum, bringing your lunch to work each day saves money and probably results in healthier eating, but it means extra time before you can get out the door in the morning and keeps you from meeting friends at that new restaurant across town. There are always trade-offs to consider!

53

Rather than pursue more money as a direct path to happiness, I suggest that you measure how your decisions relating to money and time add or subtract joy and ultimately increase or decrease the overall happiness in your life.

What makes this calculation easy is that, unlike happiness, where the metrics are totally subjective and often change, time and money are absolute and quantifiable. There are 24 hours in each day and 100 cents in every dollar. You know how many hours you work each week and what you are paid for your efforts. You know how many hours you need to work to afford a purchase. You also can calculate how long it takes you to make a week's worth of sandwiches or morning coffees and how much you save by staying out of the cafes near your office. *Time and money are finite - happiness is not!*

I'll argue that more purposefully directing your time, acknowledging and balancing the tradeoff between time and money can make you happier. Once you discover what truly brings you joy, to-do list management strategies ranging from prioritization and elimination to automation and delegation of activities can help free up time for what truly matters to you.

We will explore these topics in more detail in later in the book.

Exercise #1: List What Brings You Joy

What brings you joy? Cooking and indulging in a favorite meal, winning an award for a project at work? Watching a child learn something new? To guide your thinking, I offer Buetner's observation that finding *happiness usually involves pleasure, purpose, or pride. It's imperative to strike careful balance between these 3 Ps.* If every day is consumed with leasure and you have no real pride in what you do, then there is no real urpose in life and you will not be happy. On the other hand, if you spend ll of your time doing for others, completely consumed by your work or, vithout time for simple pleasures, you will also be unhappy.

As you complete the list below, try to be as specific as possible. Rather han writing "the holidays," list "enjoying a Thanksgiving dinner at home vith my friends and family." Rather than "my grandchildren," write, 'when little Sarah asks me about my favorite hobbies." Also, all the better f you can zero in on the smallest moment. Therefore, the Thanksgiving neal could become "when the gravy turns out perfectly". "Travel" could >e "the time I hiked further than I ever thought possible in Montana with ny closest friend."

My Dozen Joyful Moments

1.
2.
3.
4.
5.
6.
7.
8.
9.
10
11.
12.

Now think about these collective joyful activities and small moments and answer these five questions:

- Are there any apparent themes or threads that connect your joyful moments?

- Were you with others or alone?

- Do particular places/people appear often?

- Are there activities/moments that repeat themselves or are they one-time experiences?

- When is the last time you experienced these joyful moments?

To understand what's going on in your body when you feel this joy, take a few minutes to watch *"Hacking Into Your Happy Chemicals"* from The Utopian Life. You can find it on YouTube. To summarize, our positive neurochemicals are: dopamine, serotonin, oxytocin and endorphins. Dopamine motivates us to work toward our goals and surges when we achieve them. Serotonin kicks in when we feel significant or important. Oxytocin flows from intimacy and trust. And endorphins fuel that "second wind" in response to pain or stress to quell anxiety.

We all take Positive Neurochemical Breaks, as I call them - PNBs of some sort whether we label them as such or not. These particular moments are very much under our control. You can choose to meditate, pray or simply zone out at will. Read Dilbert. Sing in the shower. Scroll through family pictures. Read your favorite poems. And now best of all – The Smiling Starfish! Stop and think -what are your PNBs right now? Maybe these mood enhancing breaks made your top 12 list maybe not. *My point is to be aware of all positive moments and experience more of them* – THINK PNB!

Lets switch gears and bring money back into the equation.

How Much Do Your Favorite Activities Cost? Your Happiness per Dollar (HPD)!

$								
$$								
$$$								

free download timemoneyandjoy.com

Whether you fill out these boxes is your choice. The key is to be at least sensitive to what you do, what it costs, and whether it's a "bargain" or not in terms of your happiness. Additionally, it would help if you went through *your monthly cash outflows thinking about Happiness per Dollar (HPD)*. I am not suggesting that you account for every dollar. That level of precision might be counterproductive to happiness. Get as precise as is helpful. If nothing else, simply *keep a mindset; What is the value in happiness for that expenditure?* THINK HPD!

If money is plentiful and the pure exhilaration of being out on the open water in your expensive boat has a huge payback, you should not feel guilty about the third row. If money is tight, aim to increase lower-cost activities in the first row of the table. As Henry David Thoreau wrote, *"That man is richest whose pleasures are cheapest."*

The Best Things in Life Are Free, Really!

Smiles

Laughter

Hugs

Sleep

Singing

Memories

Gratitude

The Smiling Starfish!

Inspirational Wisdom

"When I was a child, ladies and gentlemen, I was a dreamer. I read comic books, and I was the hero of each book. I saw movies, and I was the hero in the movie. So every dream I ever dreamed has come true a hundred times... I learned very early in life that 'Without a song, the day would never end; without a song, a man ain't got a friend; without a song, the road would never bend - without a song.' So I keep singing."

Elvis Presley, American singer, from his acceptance speech from the 1970 Ten Outstanding Young Men of the Nation Awards

How Much Time Do Your Favorite Activities Take? Your Happiness per Hour (HPH)!

< Hrs							
— Hrs							
> Hrs							

free download timemoneyandjoy.com

Like the previous HPD chart, if you don't fill out this chart, that's OK. Whether you complete or not, the chart should get you into a mindset – what is the payback in happiness for your very precious time? THINK HPH! Additionally, you should go through your calendar thinking about HPH as well.

A simple yet enlightening exercise is to make a hard copy of your calendar and annotate it with smiley faces and frowns. Are the yesses in your calendar yours or someone else's??

If time is scarce, which is so often the case during the still working/ children at home phase in life, aim to increase less time-consuming activities in the first row. *Once those 40 or more hours a week free up in the post-retirement phase, there can be too much time until you clarify what's next.* Boredom and a depressing questioning of life's meaning sometimes kicks in as you finally climbed that financial mountain and the view isn't as spectacular as you imagined. This can be anticlimactic and disappointing for some. You may find yourself watching TV more and enjoying it less. Don't join the substantial number of people who lack a compelling reason to wake up each day. Rather *your aim should be to increase the third row of the table with your newly discovered, time-consuming, engaging, "encore" passion!* It is always about maximizing Happiness Per Hour!

Note that a large number of retirees are caregivers to their grandchildren. There is perhaps no greater joy and purpose, with daily love and laughter shaping the character of young family members, keeping you young! The financial benefit to your children can be significant, giving even more purpose to your efforts! Then again, is this what makes you happy? Families can be best in limited amounts. Debates about how to raise children are not uncommon. Free time for yourself? My advice is to think it through and reach some balance. At this point, you are certainly allowed to finally think of and for yourself. Be honest and practical while paying attention to the aforementioned "happiness" chemicals.

Do you feel more serotonin and dopamine when your grandchild asks for advice or from your work and/or charitable efforts?

How does the oxytocin from your grandchild's hug compare to the cortisol associated with missing yoga class due to baby-sitting?

Remember the neurochemicals. Cortisol is the lethal stress hormone. Dopamine motivates us to work toward our goals and surges when we achieve them. Serotonin kicks in when we feel significant or important. Oxytocin flows from intimacy and trust. And endorphins fuel that "second wind" in response to pain or stress to quell anxiety.

Let's Look Day by Day - "The Joy Matrix"

We will now focus on using the "Joy Matrix" to improve what you do, your activities. Later In the chapter, the focus will be on a far more interesting topic, your relationships, those with whom you spend your time.

s suggested annotating your calendar with smiley faces and frowns
an provide insight. Your day to day activities are not likely to show up
n your calendar however, they probably dominate your waking hours.
Vith this insight as background, it's important to dig a little deeper, to
iscover how you spend your time each day. Depending on how detailed
ou get, you may need a much larger worksheet. Maybe you already
ave a daily time sheet that can be converted and annotated with smiles.
rom experience with numerous students who have taken my classes, the
implest approach is to use my "Joy Matrix".

f you think about it, everything you do is either something "Required"
r "Your Choice" and it either puts a smile on your face or it does not.
)f course, many activities are in the "Neutral" category. Accordingly,
verything can be categorized in 1 of 6 boxes. Ideally, go through this
ategorization process in detail, filling out multiple sheets with all of your
ictivities. If that level of detail is just not going to happen for you, that's
nore than OK. You may get 80% of the result with 20% of the effort by
;imply keeping a *"Joy Matrix Mindset" by always asking, do I have to do
his? If yes, is there a way to make it better? Does this actually make me
1appy? How can I shift my time to things that do bring joy?*

JOY MATRIX

Emotion	Required / Feel Must Do	My Choice
Happy		
Neutral		
Unhappy		

free download timemoneyandjoy.com

In any case, I want you to capture your first column responsibilities by answering the questions: What's Required? (what you feel you must do), like going to work, walking the dog, preparing meals, cleaning the house, etc. You can also record your 2nd column "My Choice" activities, such as going to a movie or having a nice conversation with friends.

Often people in my seminars struggle initially with these matrices. To clarify, the Required column should be activities that you currently "feel" you must do. My Choice is everything else. Remember that putting an activity in the "right" square is secondary to simply thinking about its impact on your happiness and ultimately how to make improvements. Working out could be difficult to put in one of the 6 boxes. Maybe you feel it is a personal requirement but you can skip as you wish. Maybe you don't enjoy pushing your body at all. The after-effects, however, may be crucial to your happiness reducing stress hormones, triggering endorphins, better sleep, and feelings of progress. It doesn't matter which column, the key question is, does working out add to your overall happiness or not? If not, can you find a way to move up to a happier rating? Maybe the solution is a simple attitude adjustment. Suggestions: exercise with family or friends, listen to podcasts, play music. Tell yourself over and over again "I love doing pushups" then smile while you're doing them. This brain reprogramming actually makes pushups more palatable. Try it!

It is all about pulling, not pushing yourself. Positive internal messages work better than negative threats!

Another idea is to switch to a fun sport, you know something where keeping score motivates rather than punishes. Yes, I am a competitive guy. I have recently taken up pickleball, It is a sport that is fun to do with my family, easy on the knees, and all I break is a sweat. It also gives me a fun new group to socialize with.

But, let's get back to categorizing your time. Maybe it's easier to think of this in terms of an average week. Work is an obvious must do. If you are lucky, it's also what you want to do in the world and as a result would get a higher happiness rating. For many, the sense of belonging and that you are needed by others may be the perfect reasons to continue working. Retiring may be financially affordable but you might lose your sense of purpose. From my experience, when possible, working part-time indefinitely can be the best plan of all. This is especially true if you cannot find that new purposeful passion.

Moving on, a phone call to check in on a family member might literally be your choice but, given your sense of responsibility and your feeling that you must do it, then it belongs in the must do column. Again, the important point is its impact on your happiness and how to improve. If that family call isn't enjoyable, maybe change the script. If they constantly complain, switch the conversation to a favorite Netflix series or fond memories from growing up.

Note that I don't intend that you record short two-minute activities like brushing your teeth. Matrix entries should only be "significant" activities, however you define that.

he key here is to think about how what you do each day makes you feel - happy, neutral or sad -- and to record those activities in the appropriate ox. There is no right or wrong answer as to where you put an activity ecause it's personal. For example, visiting someone in a nursing home 1ay be depressing for one person while a similar visit could give another erson a real sense of purpose for helping others (serotonin).

'ake your time completing the matrix. This is not designed to be a 10 ninute exercise to be completed in one sitting. Rather, complete the natrix -- and those that follow -- in an iterative way and in detail. Perhaps ven observe yourself over a few weeks and take some notes about how arious activities made you feel.

Also, you should rank activities based on their *overall* impact on your 1appiness, even considering the impact of not doing the activity. For xample, as noted earlier, exercise may not be enjoyable at the moment, ut it still warrants a high rating, as it delivers overall longer term benefits. You might also consider any stress and guilt associated if you do not fulfill certain responsibilities.

In most cases, after this self-awareness, ratings change. Perhaps you are stressed while watching your favorite sports team lose yet another ballgame, yet find a sense of peace and progress when doing the dishes. Even better, make the chore fun. Remember "The Big Chill" kitchen scene where everyone is pitching in to clean up after dinner, while dancing to…

 www.youtube.com/watch?v=_ObVQPBD0Uw or www.youtube.com/watch?v=3s0TkufXA38

♪ ♫t I know you wanna leave me ♪ ♫

♪ ♫-"Ain't Too Proud to Beg" ♪ ♫ the Temptations

Sorry, I digress…. a lot.

It also may be useful to complete one matrix for your work week and another for your weekend. No doubt the busy work week will have more entries in the left "must do" column and the weekend sheet will have more activities in the "my choice" column. The reverse is likely true once you say goodbye to your employer. Most things you do then will be your choice. *Your "encore" conclusion, whatever it is, should reside at the joyful top of the "my choice" column.*

It can also be instructive to rate the activity in terms of cost and time. My idea is to let you be as detailed as is helpful. You can look at the big picture, staying with the first version of the matrix. Alternatively, you might take things down to the dollar and to the minute as you wish with the following matrix. You may want to make multiple copies of the second, more detailed, Joy Matrix version that follows with more adequate space. *Alternatively, you will find a spreadsheet at my website which you can tailor to your needs, saving multiple versions as you wish.*

JOY MATRIX - WEEKDAYS

Emotion	Required / Feel Must Do	$	Hrs	My Choice	$	Hrs
Happy						
Neutral						
Unhappy						

free download timemoneyandjoy.com

JOY MATRIX - WEEKENDS

Emotion	Required / Feel Must Do	$	Hrs	My Choice	$	Hrs
Happy						
Neutral						
Unhappy						

free download timemoneyandjoy.com

hen you review your matrices, you may have some surprises. Taking

ur dog for a walk may be a "Must Do," but it likely makes you happy

y inducing a surge in oxytocin, the "love hormone." Then, again, if it is 6

m., before a stressful drive to work and it is raining, the walk may not be

) enjoyable!

ow about watching the news? That's a choice, but if the calamity du

ur induces the stress hormone cortisol and impairs your sleep, you are

hoosing an activity that reduces your happiness. Your favorite sitcom

'Seinfeld," "The Office," "Modern Family" – what's your favorite?) may

learly be in the "happy my choice" square.

inally, when reviewing your matrix to determine what changes should

e made, try to replace "Your Choice" activities that do not put a smile

n your face with those that do. Ask yourself, ``Are the "yesses" on

ny calendar mine or someone else's? And, are there lower rated "Must

)o" activities that could be delegated, automated or intentionally

rocrastinated? Time is the most precious commodity not money (after

ou have enough) – so if you would rather play tennis or knit than mow

he grass, pay a lawn service.

ANOTHER HIGH FIVE

5 Steps to Breaking Bad Habits

1. Define what you want to change: It's corny, but there is power to writing a list.

2. Identify your triggers. What initiates...spot it before you are embroiled.

3. Develop a substitute plan: If you have time to fill, replace with something positive. Proactively, have a plan in place.

4. Get support -- family, friends, professional help.

5. Reward yourself. Celebrate your success!

My Top Matrix Takeaways

Having reviewed these matrices with many workshop participants, I'll offer a few general observations:

Activities in Required columns with a low ranking don't need to stay there. You can plan to move any low scores to a higher score. For example, maybe you are 60 and really don't like your job, but you need to work until 65 to meet your savings number. As discussed earlier, maybe you decide to follow your passion in a lower paying *avocation* now, something you would actually enjoy doing, and plan to "work" beyond age 65.

There are a number of ways to convert many secondary activities with a low rating to a higher rating. For example, maybe you would enjoy your commute more if you listened to a podcast, sang or called a loved one, listen to YouTube videos or TED Talks. You can find my favorite Time, Money, Happiness, Purpose, Charity, Habits and Health resources at *timemoneyandjoy.com*.

Hopefully, vacations or holidays in the My Choice all land in the happy box. The best part of vacations may be planning and remembering the experiences!

The upper right and lower right are often about good and bad habits, respectively. Many times the good habits like exercise are tough at first, but ultimately contribute to your overall happiness. Bad habits like too much processed sugar have immediate pleasure but you ultimately pay in happiness with a sour stomach or bad health. One beer might be upper right, several beers in the lower right.

After reading this book, I hope that there will be entirely new activities that will bring you Joy and Happiness. So we will come back to these matrices.

Let's Connect Time and Money

Often the best things in life are free or at least relatively inexpensive! You may be able to reduce overall expenses while actually increasing Joy by being mindful of your Happiness per Dollar (HPD). Remember, if you reduce outflows "Your Savings Number" goes down, meaning "Work Optional" comes sooner! In the "Accumulation/Saving" phase in life where there are too few hours in the day, it can be especially helpful to maximize your "Happiness Per Hour" (HPH). In the "Decumulation/ Drawdown" phase, without proper planning, there can be too much time!

The Best HPD Gifts:

Alexa – favorite songs all day

Beach water float w a drink holder

Credit card travel points

Membership to a museum

Go to *timemoneyandjoy.com* and send me an email with your best HPD gift ideas and I will share them!

Can You Multiply Your Time?

Across the board, most folks wish they had more time. To that end, here's some wisdom from Rory Vaden, co-founder of Southwestern Consulting and author of the bestsellers *Take the Stairs* and *Procrastinate on Purpose* on how to multiply time:

- There is no such thing as time management. There is only self-management.

- Prioritizing alone doesn't create more time.

- Time management has more to do with what you don't do than what you do.

- Automation is to your time what compounding interest is to your money

Ask yourself:

- *What can I do today that would make tomorrow better?*

- If I can't eliminate a task, can I automate it? Think online bill pay.

- If a task can't be automated, can it be delegated?

- If it can't be delegated – do it now?

- Procrastinate and then later maybe eliminate, automate, delegate…

To summarize, we live in a "more is better" world — but how much -- and what -- do we really need? Looking back on these exercises, I hope you have discovered more about what brings you joy and considered how you might "create" more time for these activities through prioritization, elimination, automation, delegation -- and possibly "intentional procrastination." Reconciling the ongoing tradeoffs that we all face between time, money and joy paves the way for better day-to-day decisions. This knowledge is also critical for major decisions. Not only will understanding your trade-offs help plan for your "encore" now but also provides a framework for the decisions you may face later such as housing changes and legacy planning. Of course if your first path isn't fruitful your second "encore" attempt will be more informed. Remember, it's a journey!

The Bottom Line: Understanding our personal relationship between time and money can make us happier.

Focus on Your "Encore"

"When you come to a fork in the road, take it."
Yogi Berra, American baseball player and manager

Now, let's focus more specifically on where you will find purpose, joy and happiness in your "encore". We will be a little more thoughtful than Yogi!

According to Richard Leider, we all seek purpose in our lives, whatever stage. He describes purpose as:

- Why you get up in the morning

- Crucial to your health and happiness

- A fundamental and universal need

- Not a luxury

Note that Richard is widely viewed as a pioneer of the global purpose movement. He has 3 bestsellers, including *The Power of Purpose*. You might consider his books as a resource for Step 2 – Identify and Explore Your Alternatives. Self-awareness Step 1, this book, remember is intended to make finding your specific encore, less time consuming, provide greater clarity and ultimately be a more successful quest. You should first understand what broad encore possibilities are realistic in terms of time and money. More importantly you should also truly understand what types of activities are likely to drive your happiness going forward. *Step 1 then should produce the first aha moment as you have narrowed endless alternatives to a just a handful of broad workable possibilities.* After self-awareness then it will be time to explore which specific encore will work for you. The resources I provide in the Appendix may help you explore specific opportunities in greater detail for *Step 2. – your second aha moment comes when your search is over and you have thoughtfully concluded -*

What's next!

Continuing to find purpose and joy is essential for your "encore". Remember in an earlier chapter, we discussed the idea of working more years but maybe fewer hours each week or doing something that despite less pay created more Happiness per Hour. Something where on Sunday nights, instead of dreading the work week, you cannot wait to get going the next morning!

Of course, at this writing, the COVID-19 pandemic has dramatically changed the employment landscape. Many have lost their jobs. And demographics, needs and trends are all evolving and very difficult to discern. For example lower overhead, home-based, Zoom-based opportunities exist like never before. This trend that COVID-19 accelerated, applies to businesses as well as nonprofits. Think about it, you may be able to keep a new enterprise running smoothly while visiting family and friends in far off places.

Pre-pandemic, Boomers were retiring from positions running non-profits at the same rate as they were leaving corporate America. This may create a real leadership void for many charitable organizations and may present an opportunity for transitioning Gen X and Boomers to move from corporate America into the nonprofit world. Again, salaries may be less, but the work may be more fulfilling if it aligns with your charitable interests.

Yet, despite the numbers retiring daily, Boomers still play a major role in the 9 to 5 world. According to a Pew Research Center analysis of official labor force data, not only were the majority of Baby Boomers (U.S. adults born 1946 to 1964) still in the labor force, but the oldest among them were staying in the labor force at the highest annual rate for people their age in more than half a century. In 2018, 29% of the oldest Boomers ages 65 to 72 were working or looking for work, outpacing the labor market engagement of the Silent Generation (21%) and the Greatest Generation (19%) when they were the same age.[8]

Clearly, there's no longer a magic gold watch moment when you stop working completely. In fact, about two in five companies surveyed were considering offering part-time work or flexible hours by 2020, which was nearly double the previous rate.[9] More older workers were becoming consultants or accepting temporary contracts with their current or former employers.

Some of us have it easier than others. Maybe you have a career that you love -- and it is something you can continue in as a consultant or part-time worker. However, many find themselves in search of a second act when their primary career comes to an end. This has led to the rise in so-called "encore careers" where people pursue new interests, often in service to their community. Things will change in the coming years as they always do. *The key is to be prepared, be self-aware, be resilient and be opportunistic. Seize those moments!*

8 Pew Research, July 24,, 2019. https://www.pewresearch.org/fact-tank/2019/07/24/baby-boomers-us-labor-force/

9 Andre Van Dam, Baby boomers are retiring in droves. Here are three big reasons for concern," Washington Post, March 1 2019.
https://www.chicagotribune.com/business/success/ct-biz-baby-boomers-retire-dollar-sense-20190301-story.html

ven back in 2014, a survey from Encore.org, a San Francisco–based innovation hub that taps the talent of the 50+ population as a force or good," found more than 4.5 million Americans aged 50–70 identify hemselves as working in "encore" careers (jobs or volunteer work in a nd or 3rd career that is primarily focused on job satisfaction rather than ompensation). Another 21 million were considering doing so.

Those numbers have only increased in the ensuing years. Not to be verly dramatic, but with such a greater number of Gen X and Boomers experiencing this transition without a roadmap, helping them find joy and happiness becomes essential for the health of the nation.

As you complete the exercise below, how many of the activities that you hink will make you happy have you done in the past week? In the last month? Over the last six months? In the last year?

Work as a planning tool. What do I (or did I) enjoy about my work?

Drivers or Motivators

- Accomplishments

- Belonging

- Competition

- Experiences

- Making a difference

- Mentoring

- Problem solving

- Recognition

- Structure

Don't Retire: Rewire by Jerri Sedlar & Rick Miner (2018)

Note there is a free exercise to download at timemoneyandjoy.com regarding the box above. *What you enjoy about your current work may be the single most important factor that will drive your encore happiness.* The exercise is essentially a work version of the Joy Matrix which recognizes there is usually a discretionary "My Choice" component to employment. Plus there are aspects of work that are more satisfying than others – you really should think about this!

YOUR FUTURE "JOY MATRIX"?

Emotion	Required	My Choice
Happy		
Neutral		
Unhappy		

free download timemoneyandjoy.com

The wonderful news is time may have shifted dramatically from the "Required" column to "My Choice". More than ever before you are the architect of your own happiness. So, where will those work and commuting hours go? Of course, it's one thing to complete an exercise on paper and an entirely other thing to experience a new lifestyle. That's why I suggest practice or trial runs. That is, you need to actually experience a lifestyle you think will make you happy.

If you plan on retiring to Florida, rent a house for a month or two and live there, as opposed to vacationing there. Living there, even temporarily, likely means adjusting your budget and making some connections in the community. You might consider spending time in your dream retirement locale in the "off season." Think of this time as a gap year for grownups. Use the time to step out of the rat race and reflect and plan for your future. As you recharge and reassess your goals, new options will likely present themselves, so try them out!

A classic mistake is underestimating the need to be close to family. Facetime helps but doesn't replace the hug of a grandchild. Promises to visit are not always met. So before you sell the family home, think it through realistically, Will you be happy? If volunteering is part of your equation, most organizations will let you first "dip your toes in the charitable waters" before making a real big time commitment.

Once you've spent a bit of time practicing your "encore" so you can avoid these kinds of mistakes, you might use the matrix exercises you completed earlier in this chapter and target them specifically to your dress rehearsal. It will be helpful to know how your activities made you feel and calculate both HPD and HPH. Why move south if you tire of golf after a few months? What if the heat of the summer makes running or walking your log too difficult? On the other hand, maybe more sunshine improves your lifestyle simply because you can spend more time outside engaged in low-cost, healthy activities. Maybe you prefer scheduled longer visits from your adult children as compared to day-to-day interactions.

HIGH FIVE

5 Rules for Living Well

A happy and healthy retirement depends on years of planning. In addition to saving, you should invest in your mental and physical health. As people live longer lives, dementia is an increasing worry. According to a Rush University Study of 1,845 participants in the Chicago Health and Aging Project and 920 from the Rush Memory and Aging Project, abiding by 4 of the 5 healthy lifestyle factors cuts dementia risk by 60%:

- Do not smoke

- Exercise at a moderate to vigorous level for at least 150 minutes a week

- Enjoy a brain-supporting diet

- Drink alcohol moderately

- Engage in late-life cognitive activities[1]

The key is to maintain, or improve on, your own happiness as you transition to the next stage in your life. Then you can watch that happiness increase as you share your new joy with others!

---

1 Linda Carroll, "Can you prevent Alzheimer's? 5 lifestyle behaviors that may help," *Today*, July 15, 2019. https://www.today.com/health/can-you-prevent-alzhei-mer-s-5-lifestyle-behaviors-may-help-t158472

The Bottom Line: Transitions are a time to reassess and reboot.

PNB TIME!

THE SMILING STARFISH ALL OVER AGAIN...

LEGS APART

SHOULDERS BACK

ARMS OPEN

A FEW DEEP BREATHS

STRETCH

AND SMILE

And a Song!!!

www.youtube.com/watch?v=hMc8naeeSS8 or

www.youtube.com/watch?v=SebH8En9ZOY

♪ ♫ **Dancing in the Moonlight** ♪ ♫

♪ ♫ **We get it almost every night...** ♪ ♫

-- King Harvest

♪ ♫ *Dancing in the Moonlight* ♪ ♫

Evaluate Your Relationships

"To be kind to all, like many and love a few, to be needed and wanted by those we love, is certainly the nearest we can come to happiness."

Mary Stuart, Queen of Scots

While our focus has been on you, it's important to recognize that research strongly suggests that happiness—throughout your life—is tied to the strength and number of your relationships. During COVID this is especially true. As others have suggested, they should replace "Social Distancing" with "Physical Distancing". Even as if hugs and handshakes are inadvisable, staying in touch via phone, facetime, zoom…is crucial. Isolation shortens life!

In his book *The Happiness Advantage*, Shawn Achor draws on positive psychology to explain how a positive brain fuels success and happiness in all aspects of life.[10]

---

10 Arthur Brooks, "Your Professional Decline Is Coming (Much) Sooner Than You Think, *The Atlantic*, July 2019 https://www.theatlantic.com/magazine/archive/2019/07/work-peak-professional-decline/590650

espite this and plenty of other research that proves we need others to be appy, Ruth Whippman, author of *America the Anxious: How Our Pursuit f Happiness Is Creating a Nation of Nervous Wrecks*, points out that ie self-help industry's guiding principle is that the search for happiness iould be an individual enterprise. In fact, Americans spend more than $1 illion a year on self-help books to "guide them on their inner journeys."[11]

his laser focus on individual happiness keeps Americans from connecting ith other people. According to Whippman, nearly half of all meals aten in this country are eaten alone. Teenagers and young millennials ommunicate more via smartphones than by having live conversations. .nd the Bureau of Labor Statistics found that Americans spend just 24 ours a year "hosting and attending social events." Twenty-four hours Vhippman laments are "barely enough to cover Thanksgiving dinner, and our own child's birthday party."[12]

Beyond incidental conversations at work or while running an errand, she ays American adults spend barely more than half an hour a day talking vith others. Whippman writes, "Compare that to time per day spent vatching television (three hours) or even grooming (one hour for women, nd just over 44 minutes for men)."

1 Ruth Whippman, "Happiness is Other People," *The New York Times*, October 27, 017. https://www.nytimes.com/2017/10/27/opinion/sunday/happiness-is-other-people. tml

.2 Ruth Whippman, "Happiness is Other People," *The New York Times*, October 27, 017.

Clearly if real human relationships are essential to our happiness, we have to do better.

Inspirational Wisdom

"Life is short, break the rules, forgive quickly, kiss slowly, love truly, laugh uncontrollably, and never regret anything that made you smile. Twenty years from now you will be more disappointed by the things you didn't do than by the ones you did. So throw off the bowlines. Sail away from the safe harbor. Catch the trade winds in your sails. Explore. Dream. Discover."

-- *Mark Twain*

So, How Social Are You?

Strong social relationships are the most consistent predictor of a happy life. Dwarfing any other factor, this finding is consistent across age, race, gender, income and social class.

So, let's look at your relationships. As with your "Required" and "My Choice," categories for your daily activities, you can score your relationships on a similar Joy Matrix. Obviously you want relationships that bring you happiness. My Choice relationships are easier to avoid if they make you unhappy. Spend more time with some people and avoid others. Most problematic are Required Relationships, with a boss or a close family member that make you unhappy sometimes.

Here, your only choices may be to practice "selective avoidance" or better yet, try to bring out the best in them to improve the ranking up to at least eutral if not higher. Remember, though, that the definition of insanity is

oing the same thing over and over again and expecting different results.

o, try taking a different approach with problematic people you know.

ull, don't push them. Make sure they feel they are heard – they are likely

hen to reciprocate. Sadly, there are people who are just energy vampires.

he best course of action here is to just avoid them, or say goodbye.

JOY MATRIX - RELATIONSHIPS

Emotion	Required	My Choice
Happy		
Neutral		
Unhappy		

As an important second step, I encourage you to evaluate the matrix using a framework I call the Relationship Control Spectrum. There are many factors that impact the rating of a relationship. However, control is often the most significant.

Your relationships will often fall into one of three categories:

- **Dependent relationships**: Because you are not in control, you may be unhappy.

- **Independent relationships**: These relationships may make you happy, but how happy can you be *if* the other person is dependent and possibly unhappy?

- **Interdependent relationships**: Here, control is shared, collaboration is key and both people are heard, happy and productive. $1 + 1 = 3$.

Categorizing your relationships can put a focus on control and can help you understand why you love or hate your boss, what's been missing from your marriage, or why you enjoy spending time with your high school friends.

Do You Need to Make Changes?

With a new or heightened awareness of what drives your happiness and how you spend your time and money, and with whom, may bring you to an epiphany that changes are necessary.

Obviously, you want to pursue what makes you happy. Again, if money is tight, aim to increase lower-cost activities. And, if time is at a premium, aim to increase less time-consuming positive activities. If time is plentiful nply do what makes you happiest for as much of the day as you can.

you have a spouse or significant other in your life, their involvement
each component of the process is paramount to success. Admittedly,
other person adds a level of complexity. The rewards could be double,
wever, when the two of you find your balance of Time, Money and Joy!

om my observation, couples often have underlying issues which
resolved in a loving and open conversation, could improve their
lationship. Otherwise, especially when tired, anger often boils over in
notional outbursts, the options available for resolution are flight, fight, or
eeze. Note that "reason" is not an option. We all know that no one ever
ins an argument. These are just my observations after a relatively blissful
) years of marriage. I do not have the training to be a marriage counselor
it if you need one, you should see one!

necessary, how do you begin to make a change? Psychologists suggest
at you slowly increase your "internal locus of control," the power you
ave to make easy, small changes. Studies show that even taking control
ver a few small actions can get you on your way to feeling better about
our personal relationships.

he Bottom Line: For all the brouhaha around self-help programs, real
appiness depends on other people.

Time for another mood enhancing Starfish??

LEGS APART

SHOULDERS BACK

ARMS OPEN

A FEW DEEP BREATHS

STRETCH

AND SMILE

If holding a smile for 2 minutes is difficult, create your own "happy thought." Mine are the still vivid memories from 20 years ago. They were of coming home after a long day turning the doorknob and hearing "daddy's home" with our 3 young children racing down the hallway with my wife close behind for some serious hug time. Here is an idea – play My Girl below while doing the Starfish.

www.youtube.com/watch?v=qEztui18cA8

www.youtube.com/watch?v=swSytFVMHuU

♪ ♫ **My Girl - I've got sunshine on a cloudy day** ♪ ♫

The Temptations

Homework: Choice Management

- Use charts as suggested earlier.

- Print out your calendar and annotate with smiley faces and frowns.

- For "non-calendar" activities, categorize on the Joy Matrix.

- Categorize relationships on the Joy Matrix.

- Pay attention to HPH and neurochemicals.

Make changes - stop doing "your choice doesn't make you happy," employ strategies to increase happiness - move up the Joy Matrix – try new things!!

Note that this chapter may have changed some of your financial conclusions from Chapter 3. How you spend your time and with whom can impact your expenses. If the changes are material, if you are further "enlightened" you may want to revisit your financial homework. The overall process can certainly be iterative. In the end however the iterations and added analysis should be more than worth the effort!

The fearless girl – what stress??

Chapter V

STEP THREE: Multiply Your Joy Through Giving

Since you get more joy out of giving joy to others, you should put a good deal of thought into the happiness that you are able to give."
-- Eleanor Roosevelt, US First Lady and political activist

There is a Chinese saying that goes: "If you want to be happy for an hour, take a nap. If you want to be happy for a day, go fishing. If you want to be happy for a year, inherit a fortune. If you want happiness for a lifetime, help somebody."

As evidenced by the number or organizations in the Appendix, your encore options are numerous - "Paid Work, Pro Bono, Volunteer, Entrepreneurship, Social Ventures...". Some of your options are with charities but most are not. In any case the common thread - the most likely path to purpose, to happiness, involves somehow helping others.

I like the advice above because it addresses the notion that finding happiness is a process that depends on our choices. Spend a little time in meditation every day and even the most stressful job can become more tolerable. Spend the money to hire somebody to shovel your snow and you have the free time you need to read on the weekend so you can enjoy participating in your book group.

You spent a fair amount of time in self-reflection in the previous chapter so you can understand the choices you make. Yes, "happiness comes from within," but we've also seen that happiness depends on your relationships with other people. In fact, your own happiness can be dramatically enhanced by sharing it with others. And transitioning to the post career stage may provide a greater opportunity for you to focus on *sharing* your time, money and overall happiness with others -- with wonderful results.

The Benefits of Giving

Advice most of us have heard since early in life includes: It is better to give than to receive. Also unlike some of the advice that we grew up with - like you need to wait an hour after eating to go swimming or that swallowed gum takes seven years to digest - science proves that giving is a path to happiness. In fact, MRI technology shows that giving activates the same parts of the brain that are stimulated by food and sex. Instead of Ben Franklin's early to bed and early to rise mantra, helping others may be the ticket to becoming healthy, wealthy and wise.

In *"Being Generous Really Does Make You Happier,"* Amanda MacMillan writes, "It doesn't take a neuroscientist to know that doing nice things for people feels good."[13] Sharing research that shows that even thinking about being generous has mood-boosting benefits, MacMillan summarizes a study published in *Nature Communications*. In the study, researchers from the University of Zurich told 50 people they'd receive about $100 over a few weeks. Half of the people were asked to plan to spend that money on themselves and half were asked to spend it on someone they knew. The researchers then performed MRI scans on the study participants to

13 Amanda Macmillan, "Being Generous Really Does Make You Happier," *Time,* July 14 2017. https://time.com/4857777/generosity-happiness-brain/

measure activity in three regions of the brain associated with generosity, happiness and decision-making.

Indeed, the study found that pledging to be generous was enough to make people happier. Those who had agreed to spend money on other people tended to make more generous decisions throughout the experiment, compared to those who had agreed to spend on themselves. The givers also had more interaction between the parts of the brain associated with altruism and happiness. Plus, they reported higher levels of happiness after the experiment was over.

Interestingly, larger gifts didn't translate into greater happiness. Planning to give even just a little had the same effect on happiness as giving away a lot. In fact, MacMillan quotes the study's lead author Philippe Tobler, a professor of neuroeconomics and social neuroscience as saying, *"It is worth keeping in mind that even little things have a beneficial effect, like bringing coffee to one's office mates in the morning."*

Other studies have found that generosity can have an even greater long-term impact, influencing both the giver's health and longevity. As Tobler points out, research has indicated that spending money on others can be as effective as medication or exercise for lowering your blood pressure.[14] Moreover, he says *there is a positive association between helping others and a longer life expectancy.* [15]

---

14 Amanda Macmillan, "Being Generous Really Does Make You Happier," *Time,* July 14 2017. https://time.com/4857777/generosity-happiness-brain/
15 Amanda Macmillan, "Being Generous Really Does Make You Happier," *Time,* July 14 2017. https://time.com/4857777/generosity-happiness-brain/

Charity Begins at Home

According to a Greek proverb, *"A society grows great when old people plant trees under whose shade they will never sit."* This effectively introduces a notion I have shared many times with clients, students and friends: the transfer of your values may be more important than the transfer of your wealth. Ironically, the later gets tons of attention, the former not so much.

In the first place, the term "wealth" tends to mean money, often larger sums of money. And for that reason, discussions about sharing or transferring wealth unfortunately tend to exclude people who give to others in many other non-financial ways. Nonfinancial but critically important ways of giving to others include: caring for family members, visiting elderly neighbors, or volunteering in their communities. It's important to value and celebrate those non-financial gifts. If, however, you are fortunate enough to have more money than you and your family need, and your values extend to charitable intent, then a family mission statement can help for your planned philanthropy.

A family mission statement can be a useful tool to outline the purpose of the family's wealth and put a strategy in place to achieve those goals. Not only will the document detail the family's shared values, it can provide a decision-making framework that can work well into the future. Generally, the entire family participates in some way in important financial decisions. Even younger children can take on age-appropriate grant-making roles. In

ct, the younger children are, when they get involved in money issues, the
reater the future success of the program in preparing the family for the
ansition of both values and wealth.

cluding your family in charitable work that interests all of you can be
ery rewarding. I speak from experience. My family's charitable mission
egan in 2008 when a teacher from an elementary school in a remote
Mexican fishing village, Chuburná Puerto, asked for the help of three high
chool students. My son Jordan was one of those students. The students
ere just 15 and 16 years old at the time, but they were inspired and
assionate. They organized a team of students, fundraised throughout
he year and travelled to the school to donate laptops, supplies and build
small library. Shortly thereafter, The World School was born. With
ordan's leadership our entire family - my wife Kerri, daughter Jenna and
on Cam have been on several family and friends bonding, educational
nd ultimately very successful service trips.

he World School (theworldschool.io) is a network of individuals
assionate about education. We believe cultivating student leadership and
reativity will lead to a brighter future. Our goal is to promote dialogue
nd facilitate innovative projects to help transform education here and
broad. Today we have helped a total of 22 schools in Belize, Canada,
Haiti, Mexico, Uganda and the U.S. While our focus is on education, your
amily might choose climate change or social justice to name just a few
auses as your mission.

Volunteering for a Charity or Nonprofit

In addition to helping others, volunteering gives you the opportunity to make new friends and get out of the house. If you don't know where to start, think about your interests and what you have to offer in the way of expertise, whether it's in marketing, finance or IT. Also, reviewing the "Joy Matrix" could lend direction. *What is it about what makes you happy now? Can you find that same driver of happiness working with a charity or nonprofit?* Note that while volunteering is rewarding in and of itself, it can also be a good first step in providing financial support to an organization because you gain first-hand insight and develop a connection.

Hopefully, the global pandemic has changed all of this only on a temporary basis. Many of these organizations have pivoted in how they use volunteers but, for most, the need is there, sometimes even more so!

Museums, hospitals and libraries are the traditional places to volunteer, but the wave of Boomers retiring has resulted in many new opportunities. For example, Senior Corps, a division of Corporation for National and Community Service, has a foster grandparents program that gives retirees an opportunity to mentor children. You can also volunteer for the National Park Service.

Musicians on Call sends volunteer musicians to hospitals throughout the United States. The Peace Corps actively seeks volunteers who are age 50 and older. And Big Brothers Big Sisters of America gives volunteers an opportunity to mentor youth who need an adult role model.

Often volunteering for an organization sparks an interest in providing financial support -- a mission that can be shared with your family.

Inspirational Wisdom:

"People often call me an optimist, because I show them the enormous progress they didn't know about. That makes me angry. I'm not an optimist. That makes me sound naive. I'm a very serious "possibilist." That's something I made up. It means someone who neither hopes without reason or fears without reason, someone who constantly resists the overdramatic worldview. As a possibilist, I see all this progress, and it fills me with conviction and hope that further progress is possible. This is not optimistic. It is having a clear and reasonable idea about how things are. It is having a worldview that is constructive and useful."

— Hans Rosling, *Factfulness: Ten Reasons We're Wrong About the World – and Why Things Are Better Than You Think"*

HIGH FIVE

The 5 Ps of Philanthropy

Derived from the Greek words "philos," which means loving, and "anthropos," which means humankind, philanthropy can be broadly defined as love for humankind. Philanthropy seeks to improve our world by addressing and solving various social problems. More narrowly, charitable giving focuses on eliminating the short-term suffering caused by these social problems. So addressing the roots of homelessness is philanthropy and feeding the hungry is giving. Working on global warming is philanthropy and funding a recycling campaign is giving. Philanthropy involves:

Passion: Choose a cause that you care deeply about.

Process: Some families meet to discuss shared values, create a mission statement with specific goals, and meet regularly to make grants.

Participation: Studies show that if you volunteer with the organization you support financially, or regularly attend their events, you are more satisfied.

Progress: It's helpful to track both the impact of your giving and the organization's progress toward its stated goals. Accountability is key.

Posterity: Getting your children involved in your charitable efforts, perhaps they will carry on your work with their children.

Donor-Advised Funds Can Make Giving as Easy as it is Fulfilling

How will you fund your family's mission? In my view, opening a donor-advised fund (DAF) is one of the best ways to accomplish both your short- and long-term philanthropic goals. DAFs are tax-advantaged investment accounts used for charitable giving. Around for nearly a century, DAFs were originally administered community foundations. DAFs became popular in the 1990s when major fund companies, universities and harities themselves joined the administrative ranks.

he opportunity for investment firms is obvious. Over the next 25 years, 1e Boston-based Cerulli Associates estimates that Boomers will pass .early $48 trillion in assets to their heirs and charities. Generation X will •e the biggest beneficiary. Overall, Cerulli finds that $68 trillion will be ransferred by U.S. households over the next quarter century.[16] This has •een described as the largest wealth transfer in human history. We can also •iew it as the greatest opportunity for philanthropy in the modern era.

National Philanthropic Trust' 2019 Donor Advised Fund Report finds hat in 2018, philanthropists recommended grants to charities from their lonor-advised funds totaling $23.42 billion -- a new high and an 18.9 •ercent increase from a revised 2017 total of $19.70 billion. The same apid growth also applies to contributions to donor-advised funds, which otaled $37.12 billion in 2018. This represents an 86 percent increase in :ontributions over the past five years.[17]

When you think about it, DAFs have democratized philanthropy, essentially making the charitable foundations of the rich and famous available to all of us. NPT data shows a high volume of DAFs being •pened with lower account balances. People are using them for :rowdfunding and workplace giving. The growth of DAFs in the U.S. •eflects the importance and value Americans place on philanthropy, ;omething I hope the pandemic will not upend.

---

16 Cerulli Associates, The Great Wealth Transfer 2018
17 National Philanthropic Trust *2019 Donor Advised Fund Report, 2019*

My wife Kerri and I have a DAF. Not only does it simplify our giving but it's helped us to get our children involved in philanthropy. We make "lumpy" contributions and "smooth" distributions. For tax reasons noted in "5 Steps" we donate appreciated investments every few years and then as a family decide which charities *each year* will be the recipients. Our custodian keeps ongoing detailed records. The transfer of securities from our brokerage account and the distributions to the charity could not be simpler. *In some cases (talk to your tax person) the tax savings can approach 50%.*

HIGH FIVE

5 Steps to Giving with a DAF:

Open a DAF with cash -- or other assets like appreciated stock. While most donor-advised funds require a $2,500 to $5,000 minimum initial contribution, there is typically no minimum account balance going forward.

Make your charitable grant right away, or wait. Either way, your contribution qualifies for an immediate tax deduction. Note that it will not actually save you taxes unless you are itemizing on your tax return for the year contributed. Some people will "bunch" several years worth of contributions into 1 year so that they do itemize for that 1 year. Note that if you are contributing an appreciated investment you will not have the potential tax liability associated with the gain had you sold the investment.

Consider if you want to invest your DAF assets in ESG (environmental, social, governance) to basically **do good until you do even more good upon distribution.**

Choose any IRS-approved charity when you're ready to make grants.

Review your plans with your financial advisors and tax person. It's important to understand all the DAF details in context with your tax situation and estate plan.

One last consideration – people often let the funds sit in DAFs for many years. It may be they haven't had time to research or are simply indecisive as to which charities. They theorize that the funds will grow such that more will be given later. This is true but let us not forget the benefit associated with putting money in the hands of your charity right away. Often the need is great and funding delays are costly to their mission. *The "compounding price" to the charity may be greater than the "compounding accumulation" in the DAF!*

Welcome to Planned Giving

In the financial planning world, we call what develops from opening a DAF planned giving. Rather than be motivated by an email that urges you to donate to a charity, you and your family spend time in advance trying to explore and prioritize the causes that matter most to you.

If you think your charitable giving will be too small to matter, think again. When researching the systemic structural issues that currently impede the growth of planned giving in the US, Jennifer Xia and Patrick Schmitt, students at Stanford's Graduate School of Business, found that although most organizations ignore small donors to pursue more "major gifts", small-dollar donors make up the lion's share of planned giving at most organizations. For example, one large environmental organization receives 70 percent of their planned giving dollars from people who are not part of their top 10 percent in donations.[18]

18 Jennifer Xia and Patrick Schmitt, "Philanthropy's Missing Trillions," Stanford Social Innovation Review, Stanford University, October 2017

Significantly, the researchers also found that Baby Boomers avoid estate planning. They write, "Of the 150 people surveyed between the ages of 53 and 71 who had made a contribution to a nonprofit in the last year, only 8% had a bequest or other planned gift in their estate plans. Strikingly, nearly half (47%) said that planned giving was not an option because they had no estate plan at all."[19]

Here's a really interesting part of the Stanford study, the most common words the surveyed Boomers used to describe the estate planning process were "scary," "complicated," and "expensive." Common refrains were "I don't know where to start" and "I just don't want to think about it."[20] Sound familiar?

You have plenty of company on this island of denial. There are advisors who don't check that clients have a will and estate planners who avoid philanthropy. In fact, the Stanford researchers note that nearly all of the donors they interviewed who had completed an estate plan with an attorney or online said charitable giving was not discussed during that process. And yet, with the record-setting transfer of wealth in the coming decades, planned giving could be a powerful source of funding to a range of organizations that work to improve the world.

So, how do you get philanthropy discussions rolling? In most cases, when clients begin to think about any kind of charitable giving, we have an

19 Jennifer Xia and Patrick Schmitt, "Philanthropy's Missing Trillions," Stanford Social Innovation Review, Stanford University, October 2017
20 Jennifer Xia and Patrick Schmitt, "Philanthropy's Missing Trillions," Stanford Social Innovation Review, Stanford University, October 2017

itial discussion about taking care of their family. Often, conversations bout how much clients will leave their children begin like this, *"I want y kids to have enough to be able to do anything they want in life but not) much that they do not want to do anything meaningful at all."* Here, it's nportant to look at the big picture and gauge timing for any gifting.

ou should move at a pace at which you are comfortable, and one that orks for your family. One client who was worth millions, way more nan his work optional savings number, used to spend a lot of time omplaining about his brokerage firm charging $14 for check writing and ther seemingly unimportant issues. His kids were all struggling a bit nancially, 2 were driving deathtrap cars to jobs they hated. During our ork on how to maximize family happiness, it became obvious that he hould gift to his children immediately. There are also clients who arrive t this conclusion on their own. One client's greatest joy is that their ntire family comes over almost every Friday night to a much-larger-than-hey-need home for dinner – with no screens allowed. And when each randchild reaches a certain age the grandparents take them on a trip to the lestination of their choice. Other clients and their families are very active n worthwhile charitable causes.

haring both financial information along with what drives your general lappiness with your family could be what's missing from many estate blans. That is, although families invest plenty of time and money engaging state attorneys to manage how to leave their assets to their heirs in an equal and tax-efficient way, there is often plenty of stress and strife when that time comes. I believe that's because the heirs are very often unprepared to receive the wealth.

That is, estate plans are more likely to succeed if your wealth is put in context, by sharing with your children how you were raised, how you earned your money and the causes you have supported financially throughout your life. This process is effective for all families, no matter their net worth. Yet, while it sounds simple enough, these talks rarely happen. Parents don't want to talk about their death. And, of course, money is still somewhat of a taboo subject, even among family members.

Note that my focus here on estate planning is not to suggest that you should wait until your children are grown to discuss money. Perhaps at this point in your own planning, the following advice is something you can share with your children to help your grandchildren: Despite people's insistence to the contrary, there are all kinds of natural opportunities to tal about money. These may be as simple or routine as a visit to the bank or grocery store, shopping online, planning a vacation, paying bills, mailing birthday gift, etc. And, of course, household chores, an allowance and firs jobs all afford you a useful springboard into financial topics.

5 Steps to Discussing Your Estate Plan with your Children

Whatever the value of your estate or your charitable intent, my advice is simple:

Have an honest first conversation. Discuss your values and let your heirs know at least generally the value of your estate and the outline of your plan.

Meet again, perhaps annually. Get together to encourage questions and facilitate planning.

Educate your heirs. Provide basic financial education to facilitate your heirs' future decisions.

Update and revise. Revisit your estate plan at least every couple of years.

Explain your decisions in a letter. Especially with complex estate plans, ensuring that your heirs understand your decision-making process can help to avoid any future confusion and family discord.

espite the best laid plans, many times children learn about their parents' ealth, however large the estate, only after the parents pass away. In fact, 4% of Americans who have at least $3 million in investable assets have ot talked to their children about their wealth or never will, according a Merrill Private Wealth Management's 2018 study. The survey also und that respondents did not bother to talk about their wealth with their ildren because they assumed the children had already figured it out. Yet, 7% of the survey respondents had quietly made gifts in a trust or set aside oney in their children's names.[21]

Bank of America press release, "Heirs in the Dark about Family Wealth Decisions," ly 31, 2019.

Another study by the Spectrem Group found that among Boomer investor who inherited at least $500,000, only half had taken steps to make their wealth transfer easier for their beneficiaries. In fact, 37% anticipated that there would be disputes among their beneficiaries.[22]

The most successful estate plans begin with the parents teaching their children early on that money is a means to an end and not an end in and of itself. But that's a subject for another book.

The Bottom Line: It honestly is this simple: It is better to give than receive. And that goes for your values as well as your assets.

22 Larry Swedroe, "Why Are Baby Boomer Wealth Transfers Failing?" *Advisor Perspectives,* August 24, 2019

Chapter VI

Summary:

'Thousands of candles can be lit from a single candle, and the life of the candle will not be shortened. Happiness never decreases by being shared."

Buddha

consider "Your Encore" as a retirement planning "bridge book." It bridges the essential "when should I take Social Security/ROTH conversion" type financial books with the enlightening "finding purpose/ leading the good life/managing your time" books.

As stated in the Preface my intent is to address Part A – Gaining self-awareness before Part B – Identify and Explore Alternatives. The idea is to give you an eye-opening shortcut considering the multitude of directions you could go – see "Your Encore" Resources in the Appendix for Part B help.

"Your Encore" has a relatively simple, hopefully enjoyable and just possibly epiphany - inducing approach to help you deliberately do something that you have probably been "winging" your entire life – balancing time, money and joy when making decisions!

Greater self-awareness is key at this major inflection point in your life and hence the focus of "Your Encore." Yes, time and money are finite – happiness is not!

I'm hopeful that the framework you build for Your Encore will help you to stay engaged in whatever keeps a smile on your face. For some it may be immersion in an activity – painting, golfing, reading.

However you choose to fill your days, like many folks you may find you can magnify your joy by integrating this simple advice - *If you want to be happy, help others in some way!*

Of course, your giving doesn't have to center around money or formal charities. As discussed in Chapter IV, all across the country grandparents caring for their grandchildren are molding the character of the next generation by passing along their values and keeping the grandkids safe and healthy, while also reducing stress for the parents.

Whether you give time, money or both, you can help others and increase your happiness by first forging a personal connection. Often, it is not *how much we give that matters most, but what motivates our giving. A good way to cultivate this personal connection is to draw from the exercises you completed in this book to target your key interests. For example it can help to be involved as a volunteer before donating money to a charity.*

You should also keep in mind that there are plenty of informal ways to help others without donating large amounts of time or money. To quote Aesop, *"No act of kindness, no matter how small, is ever wasted."* It can be easy to help someone in need. Simply bringing a meal to an older neighbor or having a chat over a cup of tea could make a positive difference in their lives. Also, if you can't contribute time or financially to an organization, maybe someone else can. Be a connector. If you feel passionately about a particular charity, raising awareness about it can get resources to flow their way. You can use social media or blog to promote issues you care about. You can introduce lonely neighbors to each other if you don't have the time to keep them company.

Whether you give time or money, or in large or small amounts, the key to success is to create an approach to giving that reflects who you are -- and one that works for your family. Remember, family happiness optimization is what this journey is about!

For some of you, our three-step Time, Money and Joy planning process will be completed quickly. For others, it could take much longer to fill in the blanks introduced in the Preface.

- I will fill my available time of _____ hours a week while fulfilling my obligations to others and myself.

- I can do this within my projected budget of $_____ or I need to earn/save an additional $_____.

- I will be excited to wake up every day because_____.

The deeper you go into the steps the more precisely you can fill in the blanks.

1. Identify your post career lifestyle number and if needed your savings accumulation number.

2. Align your time and money with what you value/love to create joy and happiness.

3. Share your happiness and resources to help others -- and create even greater happiness.

I hope you carefully do all of your homework and have read at least Chapter IV slowly and thoughtfully. If not, that's okay. You have started the process. If you can establish at least a few new mindsets, your happiness should improve. As a result, this book's purchase and the time you spent reading "Your Encore" will prove to be a very good decision!

Mindsets to remember:

- Choice Management
- Savings Number
- The Joy Matrix
- HPD Happiness per Dollar
- HPH Happiness per Hour

In conclusion - don't close that curtain ....

The lights are flickering - the audience wants more! You want more! *It is time to savor that limitless applause!!*

Let us end on a high note with Johnny Nash.

 www.youtube.com/watch?v=NkwJ-g0iJ6w

www.youtube.com/watch?v=FsclgtDJFXq

♪ ♫ I Can See Clearly Now ♪ ♫

Appendix:

"Your Encore" Resources:

Communities, Paid Work, Pro Bono, Volunteer, Entrepreneurship, Social Ventures, Philanthropy, Books

(Note these resources were compiled with the help of Doug Dickson. Doug is the Board Chair of Encore Boston Network. He was previously President of Discovering What's Next and the Life Planning Network. In 2010, he co-founded the national Encore Network and remains on the Leadership Council. Doug authored "Discover Your Encore".)

"Whatever community organization ... you will get satisfaction out of doing something to give back to the community that you never get in any other way."

Supreme Court Justice Ruth Bader Ginsburg

Encore Communities:

Encore Network
https://encorenetwork.org/
Find local organizations and fellow travelers you can connect with for encore programs and opportunities.

Gen2Gen (encore.org)
https://generationtogeneration.org/
Find people and organizations that are connecting the generations to help kids thrive.

The Transition Network

https://www.thetransitionnetwork.org/

Find chapters of professional women around the country who are making the encore transition together.

Project Renewment Groups

https://www.renewment.org/

Groups of career women supporting one another through the transition from work to retirement.

Life Planning Network

https://myredstring.com/lifeplanningnetwork/

Professional community of life planning coaches, career counselors, financial advisors and other professionals that advise people over 50.

Encore Work:

Note: While many people think about working or volunteering for a nonprofit in their encore years, many also work for mission-driven or purposeful businesses, many of which specifically designate themselves as having a double or triple bottom line or as "benefit corporations." Any business that serves a social purpose, and there are many, could be as much an encore choice as nonprofits. In addition, many people go into government service, either as paid staff, elected officials or serving on state or municipal boards, commissions or as volunteers. Local government positions are often posted on the town website.]

RetirementJobs.com

https://www.retirementjobs.com

Companies like RetirementJobs.com are filling a void by helping older workers keep their skills and expertise on the job.

Idealist

https://www.idealist.org

With more than 120,000 nonprofit organizations and 1.4 million monthly visitors to its English and Spanish sites, Idealist is a non-profit clearinghouse that helps people move from intention to action all over the world.

RetiredBrains.com

https://www.retiredbrains.com

This non-profit Jobs Center has both paid part-time and full-time jobs and unpaid Board of Director openings.

Commongood Careers/Koya Leadership Partners

https://koyapartners.com

This search firm places directors and managers into nonprofit organizations.

The Philanthropy News Digest

https://philanthropynewsdigest.org/

This Jobs Board has openings at foundations and nonprofits.

The National Council of Nonprofits

https://www.councilofnonprofits.org/nonprofit-jobs-and-careers

Here you can search by keyword, field, location, salary, level, (entry, experienced or internship) and required education.

The Chronicle of Philanthropy

https://www.philanthropy.com

The Jobs page lists opportunities in fundraising, executive, programming and administrative areas.

Encore Pro Bono and Volunteer Service:

Points of Light
https://www.pointsoflight.org/for-volunteers/
Listing of local and statewide organizations that match volunteers to nonprofits.

All Hands and Hearts
https://www.allhandsandhearts.org/
Recruiting site for volunteers to respond to natural disasters, offering both immediate relief and longer term recovery support.

Americorps
https://americorps.gov/
Short and long-term volunteer service opportunities to meet pressing challenges in local communities.

Peace Corps
https://www.peacecorps.gov/
Extended international volunteer opportunities in health, education, entrepreneurship and more. Couples welcome.

Teach for America
https://www.teachforamerica.org/
Extended commitment to teaching in grades K-12 in local school districts.

[Note: Many local schools and colleges will hire transitioning professionals directly into full-time, part-time and substitute positions if certain learning and certification requirements are met.]

Executive Service Corps

https://www.escus.org/

National network of local organizations that provide consulting, coaching and other services to nonprofits, schools and government agencies.

Inspiring Service

https://inspiringservice.org/

Locations where this new platform is up and running to help people find their ways to help.

Volunteer service listings

If still working, check out volunteer options through:

Volunteer Match - https://www.volunteermatch.org/

Idealist - https://www.idealist.org/

Create the Good - https://createthegood.aarp.org/

Local United Way -see local website

Catchafire - https://www.catchafire.org/

Common Impact - https://commonimpact.org/

Freelance, Remote and Flexible work options - see those listed at https://encorebostonnetwork.org/

Encore Entrepreneurship and Social Ventures:

Work for Yourself@50+

https://workforyourself.aarpfoundation.org/

Business startup toolkit from AARP Foundation.

SCORE
https://www.score.org/
Find business mentors, workshops and other startup support.

SBA Encore Entrepreneur
https://www.sba.gov/sites/default/files/2018-02/Encore_Entrepreneur_Checklist.pdf
Checklist for starting your own business with links to SBA resources.

Founders Over 55 Club
https://www.foundersover55.com
Collegial community of business founders and entrepreneurs in encore careers.

Note: Many people start projects that serve a short-term or longer-term need in their communities or elsewhere in the world, but are not nonprofits or businesses. These can be independent initiatives or formed in partnership with existing organizations.]

Encore Philanthropy:

Social Venture Partners
https://www.socialventurepartners.org/
Donors pool their funds and make collective decisions about which nonprofits and social enterprises to invest in, while offering their skills and support services for greater impact.

GuideStar USA, Inc

https://www.guidestar.org/

An information service specializing in reporting on U.S. nonprofit companies. In 2016, its database provided information on 2.5 million organizations.

Charity Navigator

https://www.charitynavigator.org/

Founded in 2001, Charity Navigator has become the nation's largest and most-utilized evaluator of charities. In our quest to help donors, our team of professional analysts have examined tens of thousands of non-profit financial documents. We've used this knowledge to develop an unbiased, objective, numbers-based rating system to assess over 9,000 of America's best-known and some lesser known, but worthy, charities.

GoFundMe

https://www.gofundme.com

Lists well-known and top-rated nonprofits that have branches across the US. It also shares resources that can help you find additional local charities and ways to give back.

Donor Advised Funds

Many financial institutions sponsor donor advised funds which may provide significant tax advantages when donating securities that have appreciated in value. Post contribution the positions are sold, invested and held until the donor directs contributions to IRS qualified charities.

Encore Books:

Encore Career Handbook: How to Make a Living and a Difference in the Second Half of Life - Marci Alboher

How to Live Forever: The Enduring Power of Connecting the Generations - Marc Freedman

Great Jobs for Everyone 50+: Finding Work That Keeps You Happy and Healthy… and Pays the Bills - Kerry Hannon

Second-Act Careers: 50+ Ways to Profit from Your Passions During Semi-Retirement - Nancy Collamer

Never Too Old to Get Rich: The Entrepreneur's Guide to Starting a Business Mid-Life - Kerry Hannon

Ageless Startup: Start a Business at Any Age - Rick Terrien

Discover Your Encore - Doug Dickson

Life Planning for You - George Kinder

The Bottom Line

As we've learned, your time can be even more valuable than your money!

Working with a Financial Advisor:

Many individuals purchase financial planning software or access other resources to help them make more informed financial decisions. If you are uncomfortable or unwilling to do your own financial planning -- including the analysis necessary to calculate "your savings number" -- I suggest you find a "fee-only" advisor. This is an advisor who never receives commissions. Commission based advisors may be less inclined to do the analysis needed. Fee-only advisors may be paid on a percentage of assets under management basis, charge hourly, or have a set fee of some sort. A big issue is whether you want an advisor to go beyond your financial planning and also manage your investments, and, if so, whether the assets you want to have managed meet the advisor's investment minimum.

Keep in mind that some advisors are fee-only and some are fee-based, which means they *may* receive commissions in addition to fees for asset management. You can find out how the advisor you are considering is paid and review their qualifications in detail by visiting the SEC's "Check Your Investment Professional" at SEC.gov | Check Your Investment Professional.

Note that I have been teaching workshops entitled *"Do It Yourself or Hire a Financial Advisor"* for several years for community education and council on aging groups. Some advisors are more than worth their fees. Others not so much! And many people with the right resources, right temperament and enough time can go it alone.

Having worked for 30+ years as both a manager and as an advisor at both large financial institutions as well as smaller boutiques, I know that my industry can be quite challenging to navigate. There are many subtle conflicts of interests as well as the more obvious conflicts. An advisor's business motivations can, even unintentionally, collide with what is best for the clients they serve.

If you would like my help to determine your best financial planning route, **Register today for "Do It Yourself or Hire a Financial Advisor" webinar at** timemoneyandjoy.com. It will be my pleasure to help you assess your goals and to prepare a list of the most important questions to ask advisors.

Note To Financial Advisors:

Dear fellow advisors:

If your clients want to maximize family happiness, their basic quest should be how to reconcile time, money and joy on a day-to-day basis and when life's crossroads surface. I believe as their trusted advisor you can help clients "create" more time for what brings joy, alleviate financial stress, and discover greater HPD (happiness per dollar) and greater HPH (happiness per hour). This process can help clients to better understand the basis of informed decisions, Their Savings Number! This magical figure can be difficult for some people to calculate on their own since so many variables are involved. Doing the work together can lead to better planning and greater happiness.

Gathering additional facts around how clients spend their time and what makes them happy can both enhance your relationship and establish a useful and systematic approach to address future family decisions. With you in the "driver's seat", clients can more easily navigate life's roadmap

In addition to helping your clients, integrating the Time Money and Joy analysis into your own life and into your practice may give you further purpose to drive your own happiness. And by differentiating you in the marketplace, it can help grow your business. Going way beyond most other advisors, you can be a hero with "how to be happier on less money and with more free time."

Adding my Time, Money and Joy steps into your financial planning process is relatively easy. I have taught these concepts to groups of appreciative advisors for the last few years. Nothing is "rocket science." In fact, most of the content seems fairly obvious after the fact. Guiding clients does not require a large investment of your time. You can simply suggest clients go through activity and relationship exercises to determine what drives their happiness and where their time goes. You can then assist as they revisit their budgets and calendars to make any appropriate changes.

Like most problems, the solution to improving financial decisions and increasing happiness invariably resides in better systems - which I thoughtfully provide! There is no requirement to delve into areas where you are untrained or uncomfortable. However, you should go through the

ime, Money and Joy process yourself first, for your own benefit as well
; your family's.

/hile "Your Encore" is targeted for a specific demographic of people
ying to figure out what's next after their career, balancing time, money
nd joy however is critical in all stages in life. This balancing act is crucial
) most financial decisions such as career choices, buying a home, gifting,
le of a business etc. Most clients would benefit by integrating time and
appiness into their financial planning and decision-making.

eviewing the six-step CFP financial planning process underscores how
aturally evaluating time, money and joy can fit into your work with
lients:

ix Step Financial Planning Process

1) Determining your current financial situation. Go beyond the
umbers, gathering information on what makes clients happy and what
oesn't. This requires clients' personal awareness and may require
iscussions among family members to reconcile any differences. See
Activity/People Joy Matrixes" and suggested homework in Chapters III
nd IV.

)etermining how time is spent will require some level of time awareness.
his can be as simple as having the client annotate their calendars with
miley faces or frowns. See suggested homework at the end of Chapter IV.

(2) Developing financial goals. To determine a client's targeted Savings Number, a financial calculation needs to be made to determine a minimal level of cash inflows necessary to cover minimum "needs" as defined by the client. Additionally, there should be a calculation of an accumulation "savings" amount needed to maintain this level of cash flow once they become "work optional"(retired). This is not simply listing current expenses and projecting them forward. This requires greater reflection by the client, factoring in what their expenses could be to obtain greater HPL (Happiness per Dollar).

(3) Identifying alternative courses of action. Now that the client is thinking about time and joy more explicitly, the alternative courses will be more informed.

(4) Evaluating alternatives. Alternatives should not only make financial sense. They should bring happiness, while managing limited time. Will alternatives bring greater HPD and HPH (Happiness Per Hour)?

(5) Creating and implementing a financial action plan. As always, a plan without action has no utility. Note that part of the action plan may involve cultivating new habits.

(6) Reevaluating and revising the plan. As crossroads in life surface, a thorough understanding of the client will allow for far more informed advice. If the crossroad involves a change in the client's main activity, a life coach or **"Life Planner" (Kinder Institute)** may be particularly helpful.

As experienced, process-oriented, financial experts with strong client relationships, advisors often become a sounding board for a myriad of life decisions. Incorporating the Time, Money and Joy process into your work will require an investment of your time upfront. You may want to try it with a few clients to start. The rewards can be wonderful, greater joy for all. Plus, getting clients focused on something other than their portfolio on a daily basis can reduce their stress and yours! If you practice what you preach and hold yourself accountable to spend your time better, what you've learned here about *Time, Money, and Joy can lead to greater client retention, new business and more fulfilling work!*

I encourage you to visit my website, *timemoneyandjoy.com* for free resources - Ted Talks, articles, books, YouTube videos on related topics that I believe you will find on point. I update the site frequently. And if you email me with additional resources you find useful, I will add your favorites to the mix.

My website lists upcoming **CPE qualified webinars**. My "engineer's" approach to happiness usually resonates with financial planners. *Can you think of more personally beneficial, fascinating or enjoyable continuing education?*

Cheers,

Glenn

Made in the USA
Middletown, DE
03 May 2022

65137906R00076